GRAND
HOTELS
OF NORTH
AMERICA

BY CATHERINE DONZEL
ALEXIS GREGORY AND MARC WALTER
PREFACE
BY PAUL GOLDBERGER

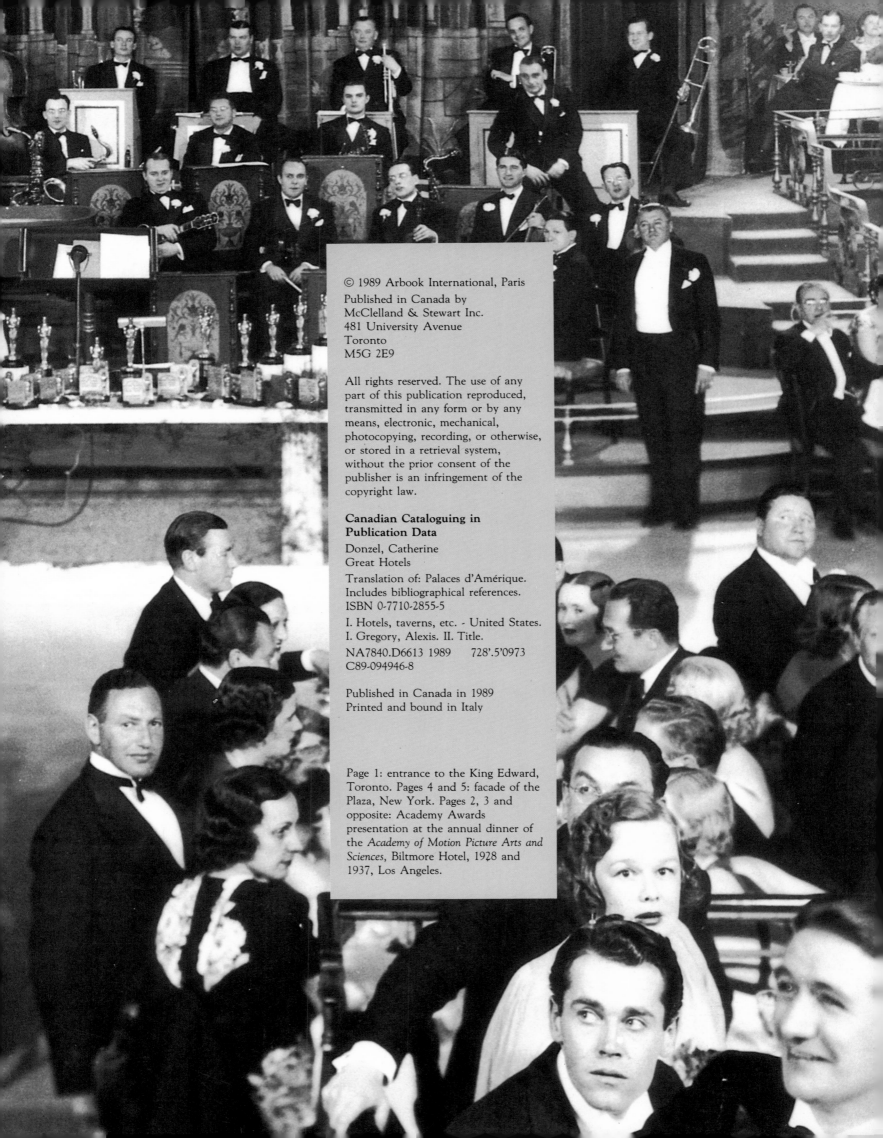

**Canadian Cataloguing in
Publication Data**
Donzel, Catherine
Great Hotels

Translation of: Palaces d'Amérique.
Includes bibliographical references.
ISBN 0-7710-2855-5

I. Hotels, taverns, etc. - United States.
I. Gregory, Alexis. II. Title.

NA7840.D6613 1989   728'.5'0973
C89-094946-8

Published in Canada in 1989
Printed and bound in Italy

Page 1: entrance to the King Edward,
Toronto. Pages 4 and 5: facade of the
Plaza, New York. Pages 2, 3 and
opposite: Academy Awards
presentation at the annual dinner of
the *Academy of Motion Picture Arts and
Sciences*, Biltmore Hotel, 1928 and
1937, Los Angeles.

PREFACE

There is something fundamentally un-American about the idea of the grand hotel: it is not democratic, it is not fair-minded, it is not for everyone. In Europe and Asia, grand hotels were always somewhere between private clubs and great villas, places that by their very nature were intended for some, not all. But it is an altogether wonderful paradox of the American grand hotel that it is, in fact, for everyone: if it is not for everyone to spend a night in, then it is for everyone to visit, to fantasize about, to celebrate in. The grand hotel in the United States and Canada has become not merely the stopping place of the rich and socially prominent but also a fantasy object for everybody else. In the North America, the grand hotel has been turned into a popular icon.

What else, after all, could we call the Plaza, the Waldorf-Astoria, the Willard, the Drake, the Palace? These hotels are landmarks in their cities, but they are more than architectural lodestones; they are institutions whose own culture has by now become inseparable from that of the cities of which they are a part. The Plaza is New York: an advertising slogan that could not be closer to the truth. Henry Janeway Hardenbergh's sumptuous French château exploded to urban scale is surely the most beloved public building in New York, for the public life led within it as much as for the architecture itself. The Plaza is where private elegance meets public grandeur, and both come off the better for it.

But so, too, with the Willard, also a Hardenbergh-designed hotel, recently restored and again a central part of the life of Washington, D.C.; or the Palace in San Francisco, by Trowbridge & Livingston, with its splendid glass-enclosed garden court, the epitome of Edwardian grace blown up to American commercial scale; or Schultze & Weaver's trio of skyscraper hotels in New York, the Waldorf-Astoria, the Sherry-Netherland, and the Pierre. The latter proved that the glory of the grand hotel need not be incompatible with the romantic joy of the skyline — indeed, that hotels could even in themselves become the skyline. (Until McKim, Mead & White's majestic, peak-roofed Savoy Plaza was torn down in the 1960's to make way for the General Motors Building, grand hotels really were the major punctuation marks on the skyline all around Central Park.)

It is no accident, surely, that the American grand hotels tend to be much larger than their European and Asian couterparts. For the very goal of the grand hotel in the United States was to mix traditional elegance with a characteristic American love of bigness. American grand hotels were almost never great urban mansions or country houses turned to a new use; they were commercial buildings, built to be hotels. If few American hotels consequently ever have had quite the opulence of the Ritz or the service of Claridge's, they managed to do something that neither of these European hotels could ever do, which is to stand as major presences on the cityscape, and as focal points for the lives of their cities. In this sense, American hotels are almost more like the grand hostelries of Asia: the Plaza or the Waldorf-Astoria for a long time played a role in New York that is a bit more like that of Raffles in Singapore or the Taj Mahal in Bombay than that of the Ritz in Paris. At its peak of perfection — in the years when its towering suites were home to Cole Porter and the Windsors, and all of New York surged through the Art Deco lobbies and ballrooms beneath them — the Waldorf-Astoria was grand hotel, monument, and gathering place: the Ritz, the Arc de Triomphe, and La Coupole, all rolled into one.

The Waldorf gets somewhat short shrift in many histories of American hotels, in part because it is the second hotel of its name; the first Waldorf-Astoria, formed by the combination of two hotels designed by the master of turn-of-the-century hotel architecture, Henry Hardenbergh, was torn down to make way for the Empire State Building. If the first Waldorf had survived it would undoubtedly be one of the city's treasured landmarks. But the "new" building, now itself more than half a century old, is one of midtown Manhattan's finest Art Deco skyscrapers. And it is really the building that empitomizes the American grand hotel, for here, more than anywhere before or since, was opulence created on a large, commercial urban scale. The Waldorf-Astoria is a skyscraper city: 42 stories high, with ballrooms, shops, nightclubs, restaurants, a theater, and even a private underground rail siding. But for all its vast size, it was as elegant as any hotel made in the early decades of the 20th century, proof that skyscraper scale need not overwhelm all aspects of hotel style.

Not all of the grand hotels in the United States have been on the scale of the Waldorf. Some of the finest are relatively small: the Art Deco hotels of Miami Beach, which are best thought of as an agglomeration than as single buildings; the Jefferson in Washington, D.C., the Hotel Jerome in Aspen, the Bel Air in Los Angeles. And then there are the vast and rambling resort hotels that are as characteristically American in their horizontal sprawl as the Waldorf is in its vertical thrust: the Hotel del Coronado outside of San Diego, the Arizona Biltmore in Phoenix, the Grand Hotel in Mackinac Island, Michigan.

Hotels have been among the only places in which Americans have been comfortable living the public life, and admitting to urbanity. Those things that make cities special — activity, congestion, continual visual stimulation, surprise — are not particularly beloved by Americans; we are a culture that by and large disdains its cities, wishing them ill and plotting our escape from them. But with hotels, all is forgiven. The intense energy of New York that so offends the Midwesterner on general principle excites him when he stays at the Carlyle; the built-up quality of Denver that disturbs the Colorado rancher pleases him when he comes to the atrium of the Brown Palace; even the private mood of Palm Beach lifts within the Breakers, for here is where the public life seems agreeable, appealing, and right. Through our grand hotels, at both cities and resorts, we recapture, at least for brief, flashing moments, the civilizing qualities of the public realm. In an age, and in a culture, that lives life almost entirely in private, traveling in metal boxes on wheels from separate houses to office cubicles and back again, an age in which even the meager public experience of attending the cinema has been replaced for many people by the private experience of television and video recorders, hotels give us some semblance of the public life. They are private places only in the strictly legal sense; in every other way, grand hotels in America are as public as the parks, places in which we are willing to lift the veil of privacy and celebrate the idea of the public realm.

Even in Los Angeles, an automobile-oriented city that can be said to epitomize the private realm in America, grand hotels have come to play a critical role as significant public places. Indeed, perhaps they are more important here than anywhere else, for there is so little else to provide a sense of the social world. So it is perhaps no accident that Los Angeles has some of the greatest of all American hotels: the Beverly Hills, the pink stucco palace that is the entertainment industry's corner tavern; the Chateau Marmont, proof that eccentricity is not without value even in the ever-more-standardized United States; and the Hotel Bel Air, the exquisite set of Spanish-style stucco buildings in lush gardens that is arguably at this moment the single finest hotel in the United States.

In all of these places, as in the best hotels anywhere, life is lived not as it is every day, but as it is envisioned, with drama and surprise, with physical beauty, and, if we are lucky, with a sense of nurturing. To elevate the public realm, to make of it something nearly perfect, to place us in a setting of physical grandeur in which everything works right: such is the mission of the grand hotels described in the pages that follow.

PAUL GOLDBERGER

Few American children have not spent rainy afternoons attempting to bankrupt their peers over a Monopoly board. Waving colored fistfuls of banknotes, they roll dice to create tiny empires of land, houses and above all hotels so pricy that one visit to Boardwalk's pale blue surface can put a rival out of business. At a tender age, future generations of tycoons thus hone their instincts, dreaming of rising from poor purple Mediterranean Avenue to a seashore empire filled with palaces and grand hotels.

In an age that reveres success to excess, possession of a palace hotel is the symbol of having arrived. In

this, American hoteliers are the stuff of legend. Conrad Hilton filled the newspapers posing with presidents and Elizabeth Taylor, his daughter-in-law. Leona Helmsley, wife of one of America's real-estate billionaires, has appointed herself a Queen and poses in a crown to advertise her husband's Helmsley Palace. Behind Chicago's Palmer House was tycoon Potter Palmer, and the elegant William Waldorf Astor is immortalized in what is surely one of the finest hostelries in the world. Ivana Trump continues a grand tradition by buzzing via helicopter between New York and Atlantic City to command her armies of chambermaids and croupiers.

THE QUEST FOR SIZE

Where power is adulated the quest for size

becomes important, and herein lies one of the great differences between American and European grand hotels. While César Ritz drove himself to a nervous breakdown refining the service and decor that made his hotels immortal, Americans aimed at building the longest, widest or tallest. Before the steel skeleton and elevator provided *height*, resort hotels in Saratoga Springs, Long Branch or Mackinac Island sought *length* with sprawling, chair-covered porches. The "longest-porch contest" was won by Mackinac's

Grand Hotel whose 700-foot veranda was supported by 40 three-story pillars. Other hotels competed to offer the most rooms, creating endless ranks of doors strung along surrealist corridors to which roller skates were more appropriate than shoe leather. When a hotel became popular enough, an annex was added, often with no architectural or aesthetic link to the parent. The skyscraper arrived in due time, spawning the eerily beautiful skyline that leaves breathless all who first greet Manhattan from the sea or from one of the heroic bridges that link it to the mainland. Hotels stretching into the heavens fulfilled a promoter's dream

1. The Book Cadillac Hotel, Detroit, Michigan. 2. The Bellevue-Stratford Hotel, Philadelphia, Pennsylvania. 3. The Cleveland (now the Stouffer City Plaza), Cleveland, Ohio. 4. The Grand Hotel, Mackinac Island, Michigan. Left page : The world's most famous hotel cityscape with, from left to right, the Ritz Tower, the Sherry-Netherland, the Savoy Plaza, and the Plaza, New York City, in 1933.

nowhere better than at that junction of New York's Fifth Avenue and Upper Fifties, where the Plaza, Sherry-Netherland, Savoy Plaza and Pierre once vied with each other, creating a romantic skyline that served as a paragon of metropolitan elegance for nearly half a century. The Savoy Plaza was replaced in the early sixties by a banal glass and steel box; but the remaining dowagers still proudly hold court. The Essex House, St. Moritz and Barbizon Plaza (located along Central Park South) were conceived in the heady 1920s and born after the Great Crash. These giant children grew up empty and hungry, but they survived as apartments for the super-rich as well as hotels for the not-so-glamorous.

Great size carries two great disadvantages. The first is fiscal vulnerability. Gigantic investments must be amortized and hefty loans serviced. While Europeans are generally faithful and habit-prone,

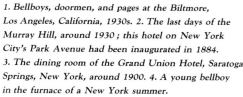

Americans adore change ; they constantly move from one new place to another. American hotels rapidly go out of fashion in a consumer society bred

to waste and extravagance. Few countries have granted such short lives to their grand hotels. An elegant resort like New Jersey's Cape May was

quickly replaced by nearby Atlantic City, leaving a sprawling wooden city empty on the long deserted beach. The small *hôtel de plage* in a *démodé* European resort might survive the vagaries of fashion, but the owner of the vast Mount Vernon, built in Cape May in the 1850s, could only pray that his useless dinosaur would go up in smoke. (In fact, so many deficitary hotels became bonfires that one wonders whether sharp owners weren't intentionally paying off mortgages with their insurance proceeds.) Some that didn't burn became apartments, offices, academies, seminaries, sanitariums or lunatic asylums. Others fell to the wrecker's ball.

The second disadvantage is deteriorating service, always a particularly delicate problem in the New World. Hotels are propaganda machines constantly proclaiming their suavity, modernity and superiority.

1. Bellboys, doormen, and pages at the Biltmore, Los Angeles, California, 1930s. 2. The last days of the Murray Hill, around 1930 ; this hotel on New York City's Park Avenue had been inaugurated in 1884. 3. The dining room of the Grand Union Hotel, Saratoga Springs, New York, around 1900. 4. A young bellboy in the furnace of a New York summer.

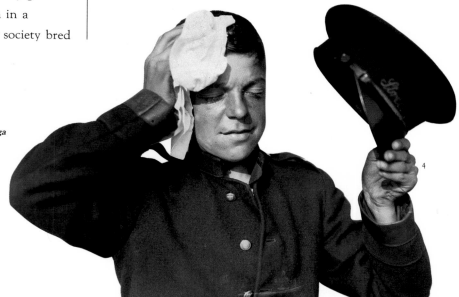

And, in truth, the early American hotels were far ahead of the European in such essentials as elevators, telephones, plumbing, gas and electric light. But these are merely mechanical services. The little we know of yesterday's servant-guest ratios gives no absolute indication of service quality, but César Ritz's reasonably sized staffs were certainly easier to manage

than the regiments of his American counterparts. One reads of American nineteenth-century luxury hotels that had a servant for every guest; one might think that this would be a guarantee of impeccable service but, alas, history seems to prove otherwise.

If hotel service today is any indication of past tradition, Americans have never been spoiled. A recent guest at a New York Hotel who sent back his breakfast told the puzzled waiter that it couldn't possibly be his, as he had waited only forty-five minutes... Constant travelers return to rooms still un-made in mid-afternoon; housekeepers crash through their doors at 8 o'clock in the morning assuming they have either checked out or died. In fact, the great hoteliers of Europe dislike having a predominantly American clientele: it spoils the staff. Americans are too generous and consi-

1. Dining room of the Grand Hotel, Mackinac Island, Michigan. 2. The St Moritz, built on the southern edge of Central Park and designed by Emery Roth, New York City, 1930. 3. A woman baggage porter (around 1940) in a New York hotel; another innovation symbolizing everything that separates the American hotel from its European counterparts.

derate; they overtip and seldom complain. They are good-natured, unspoiled and, until quite recently, were unused to pampering.

DEMOCRACY AND MOBILITY

Size is not the only impediment to good service. A country whose motto is "all men are created equal" can hardly perpetuate a servant class. The masses who left Europe's poverty and discrimination wanted no more of servitude; making beds and carrying bags are not careers to which the children of immigrants aspired. Consequently, these workers have always been drawn from America's least skilled classes.

Before World War II, European hoteliers could draw on members of a servant class to whom a fixed society, in which everyone had his place, was the norm. Being "in service" was one of many trades, and all good European hotels had husband-and-wife teams working as valet and maid. Downstairs was their way of life; in the United States, everybody ran for the staircase.

America's democratic society contributed to the birth of the large hotel. Until the mid-nineteeth century, rich Europeans took their pleasure in each other's castles, large houses and yachts. The few resort hotels were for a small

and privileged class, and it was mostly the rich who traveled through the great capitals of Europe. In the United States, everybody wanted to move around and to vacation away from home, and many more people could afford to. Life was far more public, and hotels devoted gigantic spaces to dining rooms, parlors and lobbies, which became centers of social and community life for the wealthy. Weddings and debutante parties, fund-raising dinner-dances and bar-mitzvahs have traditionally taken place outside the home, with the exception of a short period in which such robber barons as the Vanderbilts and Astors had houses as large as hotels.

From early days, American hotels were also centers of political life. American political candidates are all acquainted with "rubber-chicken banquets" for thousands of supporters, and the violent attacks on Robert Kennedy and Ronald Reagan, both shot at grand hotels, are embedded in the consciousness of people throughout the world.

It was not unusual to encounter early hotels whose great halls sat several hundred for dinner (it was, incidentally, once the custom to separate men and women in dining and public areas). Hence while Escoffier worried about how to present peaches to Nellie Melba, America's dining-room managers toiled to feed armies. American hotels coped by creating the American Plan, under which the room rate included four large meals a day. (The Modified American Plan, a later refinement, included either lunch or dinner. The European Plan covered only the room.) In Europe, the American Plan was called *pension complète*, but the kind of establishment offering it was the equivalent of a boarding house and certainly not a hotel, grand or otherwise. A clerk at one of New York's then fashionable hotels once innocently asked an upper-class English guest, "American or European, Sir?" only to be told that it was none of his business.

Another reason for the large hotel, particularly in town, was mobi-

lity. The United States was a growing nation with a common language, limitless space and no internal frontiers. When Europe was divided into hundreds of principalities with endless borders, Americans could board stage coaches and go wherever they pleased without passports or work permits. A huge market needed servicing, and the traveling salesman or "drummer" became a mainstay of the urban hotel. So did traveling theatre troupes, who created havoc and scandal with their bohemian habits and late dining hours (hotels that admitted them were often considered disreputable). But the true contribution of America's mobile society to world *hôtellerie* was the residential hotel. Young people seeking opportunity left the heartlands for the big cities – just as city dwellers have left the drabness of concrete to conquer green wildernesses. Wan-

derlust is the stuff of the American dream, and residential hotels gave wanderers food and shelter without the obligation of putting down roots.

Residential hotels are an essential part of the American scene and are often mixed into its great palaces. New York's Pierre, Sherry Netherland, Barbizon Plaza and Carlyle are today largely devoted to apartments filled with the art treasures of the super-rich, who are fully at home and yet can summon room service at midnight on the

1. A waitress in the Grand Hotel, Mackinac Island, Michigan. 2. A stagecoach in front of a New Hampshire hotel, around 1900. 3. The Belvedere Hotel's chef, Baltimore, Maryland, 1947. 4. The Knickerbocker, an apartment hotel in New York City.

butler's day off. They are served by the same staff that caters to the transient guests.

FANTASYLAND

Another element characterizing the American Hotel was a sense of fantasy that went far beyond anything conceived in Europe. Numerous nineteenth century hotels playfully sought to create an atmosphere of make-believe: Carrère and Hastings' concrete Spanish palace, the Ponce de Leon in St. Augustine; the nearby Alcazar, an evocation of the Moorish palace in Seville in whose swimming pool floated a Venetian gondola; Mission Inn, opened in Riverside, Californie, in 1903; or the Glacier Park Hotel in Montana, opened in 1913, whose 60-foot tall lobby dominated by two rows of huge tree trunks and decorated by a frieze depicting the history of the Black-foot tribe, is one of the most astonishing spaces in the world. The theatrical extravagance of all of these buildings testifies to a calculated desire to entertain, to whisk guests away from the problems of everyday life.

create a world without time where day and night are interchangeable, where slot machines ring twenty-four hours a day and bar girls are available for chips even after breakfast. And, of course, at the Disneyland Hotel in Anaheim, California, where parents from the entire world are dragged by their children, fantasy is also complete. One walks past sunken waterfalls, pirate coves, and Chinese pagodas to breakfast with Bugs Bunny and Snow White. At Miami Beach's Sans Souci, erected in 1948, and above all the Fontainebleau (pronounced *fountain blue* and built in 1952-4) Morris Lapidus created an endlessly curving space covered in rich marble embellished with gilt and crystal chandeliers, which he described as "French which is not French, a pot-pourri of anything I could put my hands on." In this decor, wives of rich urban profiteers parade in

chinchilla coats, sheltered from the tropical night by air-conditioning so relentless that many guests go home with pneumonia as well as suntans.

Another great fantasy architect, John Portman, took the traditional concept of a sky-lighted hall to its outer-most limits, pushing the canopy into the stratosphere, surrounding the hall with tiers of corridors draped like a hanging

Today, the tradition of providing escapist fantasy is continued by Caesar's Palace in Las Vegas. Doormen in togas, Cleopatra's barge afloat in the hall, large suites with mirrored ceilings and heart-shaped tubs

1. The Carlyle, an apartment hotel built in 1929-30, New York City.
2. The Nautilus Hotel, designed by Schultze and Weaver, under construction in 1923, Miami Beach, Florida. 3. The Tampa Bay Hotel, Tampa, Florida . 4. The underground dining room of the Grunewald Hotel, New Orleans, Louisiana, around 1900.

Babylonian garden in extravagant greenery. Space-age elevators glistening in lights propel guests to their rooms, providing endless activity and articulation as waiters circulate below with frosted drinks. It is kitsch, but it works, and Portman's hotels are largely responsible for downtown Atlanta's revival.

A GOLDEN AGE

America's first Golden Age of *hotellerie* was in the early nineteenth century, when the New World led the field and American hotels were truly a national expression.

Until the early years of the Republic, American inns were neither more nor less comfortable than their rugged English counterparts. Meals were taken with the establishment's owner and his family; washing up was often done at the stable pump; indoor sanitation was unheard of. It was common for

several travellers unknown to each other to share the same room, which was rarely locked. Unaccompanied women were turned away. New York's long-vanished City Hotel of 1794 (designed by British-born Benjamin Latrobe), with its private accommodations, ballroom and banquet hall, augured the changes to come. But it was Isaiah Rogers' technically advanced, conveniently laid-out Tremont House in Boston (1828-29) which finally set the standard for hotel design and established America's leadership in the field. Tremont House's austere, neo-classical granite facade also made it the first hotel deliberately designed as a monument. The American Grand Hotel, incorporating ample, elegant public gathering places, the latest trends in interior design, modern sanitary amenities, and a dignified architecture, was born.

The American example influenced grand hotel design on the other side of the Atlantic, and soon Europe was  tailoring New World innovation to suit Old World tradition and refinement. By mid-century, it was the Americans who looked to Europe for inspiration, and the great new ideas of design and luxury were found in Europe's Universal Expositions. The first, at Hyde

1. The veranda of the Tampa Bay Hotel, Tampa, Florida. 2. Letterhead depicting the famous trio of hotels in Saint Augustine, Florida. 3. An 1883 painting by Joseph F. Hatch showing the Bangor House (designed by Isaiah Rogers in 1834), Bangor, Maine.

Park's Crystal Palace, in 1851, drew six million visitors to London; the 1862 Exhibition in Brompton brought even more. Elaborate hotels were built to house the crowds: the Charing Cross in 1863, the gigantic Langham on Portland Place in 1864, and in 1874 the Midland Grand at St. Pancras Station. France's Napoleon III encouraged the rich Pereire brothers to found the *Compagnie Immobilière des Hôtels et des Immeubles de la Rue de Rivoli*, which inaugurated the Hôtel du Louvre in 1855. The Grand Ho-

tel, near Garnier's Opera, followed in 1862 with great public rooms in the gaudy taste of the Second Empire. Stucco and gold, great mirrors, enormous glittering chandeliers and painted panels embellished with rococo frames reflected a prosperous age. Paris led in *luxe* and inspired the great hotels of Vienna, Berlin, Rome and Cairo. Brought to America, the « Ritz style » swept many American hotels while Queen Anne and Tudor conquered others. The new resorts in Florida looked to medieval and Renaissance Italy and Spain while those in California saw Spain through the prism of Mexico. Only Chicago remained true to itself, developing the skyscraper after the Great Fire of 1871. The skyscraper revolutionized hotel construction but not style;

1. The Grand Ballroom of the Fairmont Hotel, San Francisco, California, 1907. 2. The Ritz-Carlton, New York City. 3. Renovation of the Palmer House, Chicago, Illinois.

traditional decor was simply housed in a new structure. Europe's refined food and service were still years ahead of the New World's.

The second Golden Age of American hotels is being lived today. In a homogenized world where travel is largely mere transportation, even refined old Europe has had to adopt the American formula of size and efficiency. For nearly half a century, Europe and Asia have looked increasingly to the United States. European and especially Asian chains must erect American-style commercial hotels, and a room in Kuala Lumpur is often indistinguishable from one in Kansas City. Though some of the romance of travel may be lost, better to find a clean, air-conditioned room in Kathmandu than to meet a cobra hissing in the bath or scorpions in your shoes. Today, an international American style is all-pervasive. Even many older European palace hotels have been renovated and adopted the new look.

Alternatively, internationalization has had a wonderful effect in the United States. Americans who savored European comfort resented poor service when they returned home. When Richard Nixon devalued the dollar, spoiled Europeans flocked over, expecting concierges, good food, decent room service, turned-down beds and receptionists in black tie or striped trousers. *Mirabile dictu*, they can now find them, particularly as European hoteliers increasingly take over or renovate American hotels. (Still, trusting foreigners who leave their shoes in the corridor for polishing risk going to morning appointments in their socks.)

Another contemporary refinement is the small hotel: size is no longer essential to success, and hotels such as the Mansion on Turtle Creek in Dallas or L'Ermitage in Beverly Hills are as sophisticated and

luxurious as anything to be found elsewhere. As for the gigantic hotels, the trend is increasingly swinging towards greater personalisation by breaking up interior space: a single floor might now be endowed with a concierge, private elevator, and its own room service. And where new owners once tended to ruin hotels with vulgar modernization, today's entrepreneurs painstakingly restore their palaces's past splendors. Two excellent examples are the $150,000,000 conversion of the 3,000-room Chicago Hilton and Trump's sumptuous renovation of Manhattan's Plaza. The history of America's grand hotels is, then, a living legend in size, extravagance, fantasy and fun.

THE ELEPHANT AND THE PERIWINKLE

The Golden Age of the American Grand Hotel began appropriately in New England, cradle of the new civilization. Boston's Tremont House, named after the street on which it stood, opened in 1829 with an elaborate banquet organised for the cream of New England society. It was immediately hailed as "one of the triumphs of American genius". The Tremont's luxury, elegant architecture, spacious rooms, fine furnishings and refined service had no equal in America's public lodgings. High ceilings,

mosaic floors, a reading room stocked with foreign newspapers and a bar where, Charles Dickens wrote, "the stranger is initiated into the mysteries of the gin sling, sherry cobbler, mint julep, zangaree, timber

doodle and other rare drinks" combined to make this palace the center of Boston's public life. There were one hundred and seventy rooms, and the clerk gave each guest a key to asssure privacy in a room with a real bed, proper curtains and a rug. The wonderment of the guest when the maid brought in not only his own water pitcher and bowl for washing but even a

piece of yellow soap (which, incidentally, was used for subsequent guests until it became a mere sliver), indicates how unspoiled the early American traveler was.

The Tremont made a sensation. Its elegantly simple granite facade was articulated with pilasters and its four-columned Doric entrance must have thrilled the townsfolk and even impressed the classical scholars from the college across the river in Cambridge. The entering guest was greeted no by the usual barroom, but by a colonnaded rotunda specifically designed as a lobby. The main dining room, seventy feet long and thirty-one feet wide, could seat nearly two hundred, for dinners of French cuisine made by European chefs. Six large rooms facing Tremont Street accommodated meetings and parties. All of this unaccustomed luxury does not

1. Maitre d'hotel of the Biltmore, Los Angeles, California. 2. A view of the Tremont House on Tremont Street in Boston, Massachusetts. 3. The Saint Clair Hotel, Baltimore, Maryland, shown here in 1871; founded in 1856 as the Gilmore House, this establishment was torn down in 1895.

seem to have unduly ruffled the normally restrained Bostonians, descendants of the Puritans.

The Tremont closed in 1895, only sixty-six years after its spectacular birth. To more recent generations of Bostonians and the everchanging students from nearby colleges, the Ritz on Boston Common has epitomized *luxe*; its gentility and

sparely elegant furnishings do indeed set a high standard, but they couldn't possibly have created the sensation of its pioneering predecessor.

Seven years after the Tremont came New York's Astor House, commissioned by John Jacob Astor, who had made his first fortune trading furs before becoming staggeringly rich in real estate. Astor hired Rogers to design a blatant copy of Tremont House. His choice was far from innocent: at the time, New York was striving to surpass Boston as North America's most important city, and competition between the two contenders was fierce. By choosing

the man who had designed the most talked-about hotel in the nation, Astor hoped to assure upstart New York's supremacy over its northern rival.

There were notable differences between Tremont House and the Astor: the Astor boasted nearly twice as many rooms and dramatically improved lighting, plumbing and heating. It had its own gas plant and a large steam system that sent hot water to the rooms as well as to bathing chambers in the basement.

The Astor became the stopping place of the great and mighty visiting America's largest port and business hub, but its fortunes declined as the world moved uptown. Its glory lasted less than twenty-five years.

Other fine hotels opened during the heyday of the Tremont and Astor. Boston had the American House (1835), the United States, the Adams House and the Revere House (all 1840s) and the old Parker House (1856). In New York the Astor was quickly challenged by the Howard (1839), the New York (1844), the old Irving House (1848) and the famous Fifth Avenue (1859). As the great railways expanded, excellent hotels were built in Baltimore, Philadelphia,

1. Panoramic view of Broadway with the facade of the Astor House in the center, New York City, 1899. 2. Facade (to the right in the photograph) of the Revere House, Boston, Massachusetts, around 1860. 3. The so-called 'Teddy Roosevelt Room' in the Merchant's Hotel, St. Paul, Minnesota, around 1900. 4. The Ryan Hotel, St. Paul, Minnesota.

New Orleans , Pittsburgh and Cincinnati. Noting their size, the popular British journalist George

Augustus Sala said, "the American hotel is to an English hotel what an elephant is to a periwinkle... as roomy as Buckingham Palace and not much inferior in its internal fittings".

THE FIRST RESORTS

Vast fortunes were easily made and lost in this expansive age; they were also flaunted in new luxurious resorts. Health has always been a pretext for a holiday, and such spas as New York's Saratoga Springs and Virginia's Hot Springs and White Sulphur Springs were the New World's Baden-Baden, Karlsbad and Vichy. The major difference was that in the New World brass, not class, set the tone. In Saratoga Springs, Diamond Jim Brady attracted the crowds, not the Empress Eugenie.

More contemplative Americans meditated in the Catskills, land of Rip Van Winkle and source of inspiration for the romantic canvases of the Hudson River School. These mountains, a game-rich Indian hunting ground, bordered the equally fruitful Hudson. By the eighteenth century, the river had become a major

1. The Maxwell House (built between 1859 and 1869), Nashville, Tennessee. 2. The Lake View Hotel, Asbury Park, New Jersey. 3. During the 1880s the Kaaterskill was one of the rivals of the Catskill Mountain House, the Catskills, New York. 4. The Oriental, Coney Island, Brooklyn, New York.

route between New York and the inland Towns, and sailing sloops carried passengers on day trips to admire the scenery. There were cliffs and mountains, forest and foliage, cascading waterfalls and forbidding palisades. The beauty of its setting, and the great country aeries of the tax-free rich along its banks – Olona, Boscobel, Castel Rock, Carrollcliffe, Lyndhurst, Kykuit and others – soon earned it the sobriquet "the American Rhine".

The Catskills – so close to New York but worlds away from its plagues and dirt – quickly became a popular resort area in

THE HOTEL OF THE CATSKILLS.

HOTEL KAATERSKILL.
June 25th to October 1st. 1884.

which hotels were sorely needed. The splendid Catskill Mountain House opened in 1823, right at the edge of a cliff, and at first could be reached only by foot. In the 1840s, it was remodelled in the Greek Revival style: thirteen Corinthian columns, symbolizing the thirteen original American states, and a great wind-blown American flag dominated its setting. The Grand Hotel joined the scene, and other resorts followed, some of them adopting the stylish "mountain house" appellation, including the Overlook and the Mohonk. In later years, the Catskills were filled with less elegant boarding houses that gradually evolved into such enormous resorts as Grossinger's and Brown's, which served mainly

middle-class Jewish families, most particularly those of Russian origin, from New York City. These and similar resorts achieved a certain status in matchmaking: many happy marriages can be traced back to weekends in what is known today as "the Bortsch Belt."

And of course there was also the sea. The Jersey shore first had Long Branch, then Cape May and finally Atlantic City. To all effects, none exists as an active resort today. The same is true of Brooklyn's Coney Island, whose splendid sand castles – the Brighton Beach Hotel, the Oriental, the Manhattan Beach – housed many New Yorkers who came to revel in balloon ascensions, John Philip Sousa's band and fireworks depicting "The Last Days of Pompeii."

Resorts abroad attracted European high society; once society became stratified, american hotels grew into haunts for those who were out of the running. The Vanderbilts, Astors, Belmonts, and other grandees all carried on in Newport in their "cottages" – actually ornate palaces as big as many hotels and more luxurious than most. Long Island's fashionable Hamptons, the summer haven of rich and successful New Yorkers, never had a grand hotel; sporting life there is played out in private clubs that still meticulously exclude anybody who doesn't fit the Anglo-Saxon mold, and night life is organized privately in elaborate shingled houses. Since the

beginning of this century, America has had no seaside equivalent of Monte Carlo's Hôtel de Paris, the Carlton in Cannes or the Hôtel du Palais in Biarritz, whose guests were as elegant as their surroundings. In Europe today, high society has also moved away from the hotel to the villa and chalet, but this movement came fifty years later than in America, so Europe's grand resort hotels survive intact for a new and more mobile international clientele.

In nineteenth-century America, any man with money to spend could attempt to crash his way upwards, checking into the grand hotels of Saratoga Springs and hoping to rub elbows with Vanderbilts, Whitneys or the nearest rich equivalent thereof – the people who held the reins of commerce and finance. Cigars on the Grand Union's porch might just propel an ambitious striver onto a higher plane, and his pretty wife, if she could sit next to Mrs. Vanderbilt at the Gideon Putman's Opera House, might one day take tea in the legendary Fifth Avenue mansion. In the same spirit, aspiring movie stars today lie around the pool of the Beverly Hills Hotel and have themselves paged on the telephone in the hope that their names will register with sunbathing agents and producers.

The baths were just a pretext at Saratoga Springs. Newly rich Americans, bored with the Puritan ethic, wanted to dress up, gamble, promenade and flirt in an opu-

1. A 1935 advertisement announcing improvements at the Saratoga Spa, New York. 2 and 3. The lively midsummer night's atmosphere on the veranda of the United States Hotel, Saratoga Springs, New York, around 1900.

lent setting, and "taking the waters" was polite fiction for showy self-indulgence. Three grand hotels were perfect foils for such fun; the Union Hotel (originally the Union Hall and later Grand Union), the United States Hotel and the Congress Hall.

The Union stretched 450 feet along Broadway and its colonnaded facade provided a sheltered view of the carriages and promenaders in the latest fashions. Ranged behind its windows were luxurious parlors, and a vast dining room where cotillions were held every evening. Its two wings, each a

quarter-mile long, enclosed a garden as opulent as Paris's Tuileries, where fountains played between flowered parterres and couples strolled. The wings of the hotel were devoted to townhouse-like "cottage suites" in which guests could set up housekeeping with a greater degree of privacy than that afforded in the hotel's bedrooms.

Each cottage suite contained a private bathroom,

several bedrooms and a living room. Meals could be brought in – an early version of room service. Cottagers were sheltered from the common sort in the "ordinary" rooms (and shared bathrooms) of the hotel proper. Slightly naughty or a little more so, cottage suites inspired journalist James Gordon Bennett to

describe them as "the seraglio of prurient aristocracy." It couldn't be helped: Saratoga Springs permitted casino gambling and fervent wagering at the racetrack – indeed, the track season began with the arrival of the annual Cavanaugh Special, a chartered train; it carried that famous bookmaker's *six hundred* assistants, and bands played when it arrived. But there would be no bordellos. Even so, America's great madams – Sinclair, Landay and Adams – regularly sent their finest *protégées* by train from New York, and several of these pretty "sporting girls" made spectacular marriages.

Other Saratoga Springs hotels were as grand as the Grand Union, and contemporary engravings present a delicious world of warm summer nights in the hotel gardens, terraces and piazzas, of men in checkered tail coats and boater hats with big-busted ladies listening to Victor Herbert's symphony orchestra. Seldom has hotel life anywhere so perfectly set the stage. It's all gone now, like a dream.

1. The United States Hotel in Cape May, New Jersey; this establishment would be destroyed by fire in the 1870s. 2. The Brighton Beach Hotel, Coney Island, Brooklyn, New York; this beautiful edifice, whose light-colored facade contrasted with the red of its roofs, was inaugurated in 1878. 3. The Mount Vernon, Cape May, New Jersey; built in 1853, expanded in 1854, it was then the largest resort hotel in the world.

A RACE FOR THE SUN

Whereas Baden-Baden has the Black Forest and Aix-les-Bains the beautiful mountain lakes, American resorts often had no natural attributes to exploit. This is particularly true of an area that was retrieved from swamplands to become one of the most successful winter resort areas in the world. Railroad owners Henry Morrison Flagler and Henry Plant were visionaries who saw Florida as a great appendage extending the United States into the warm Gulf Stream with its promise of endless summer. Before train tracks wended along both edges of the Sunshine State, Florida was shared mostly by alligators and Seminole Indians.

Flagler, the son of a Presbyterian minister, began

as a store clerk, married well, and – with $100,000 borrowed from Flagler's in-laws, the Harknesses – set up a business called Standard Oil with young John D. Rockfeller. By 1879, the two controlled ninety-five percent of the petroleum industry and were as rich as Croesus. Or two Croesuses. Flagler first visited Florida with his ailing wife in 1878, traveling ninety hours to Jacksonville, where the rails ended. Three years later, his wife died and Flagler married her nurse. They honeymooned in St. Augustine and

moved there in 1885, and Flagler soon launched his plan. He began a grand hotel appropriately named after Ponce de Leon, the Spanish explorer who looked for the Fountain of Youth, in Florida. In any period, Flagler's hotel would have been a heroic undertaking: because it was situated on a marsh, the enormous, four-story Spanish Renaissance structure had to be built on a foundation of thousands of pilings made of whole pinetrees. As architects, Flagler chose two young graduates of the prestigious Beaux-Arts

architecture school in Paris: Thomas Hastings, the son of Flagler's minister, and John M. Carrère. The enterprise launched not only Florida's age of luxury but the firm of Carrère and Hastings, which designed the finest monuments of its time, including the Senate and House office buildings in Washington, New York's Public Library, Henry Clay Frick's mansion, and the great houses of any fashionable robber baron who wanted an instant palace. During construction, twelve hundred black laborers mixed a special concrete consisting of cement, sand and coquina shells, giving the walls an unusual texture. The hotel had a large garden court, an eighty-foot rotunda with mosaic floors and frescoed ceilings, 450 guest suites and a dining room for 700 with a musician's gallery. Tiffany made the chandeliers and stained-glass windows; wood paneling was brought from New York; and draperies, carpets and furniture came from Europe. With its stuffed furniture, dripping stucco ceilings and

walls embellished in gold, the giant hotel fell somewhere between the Roxy and the Titanic. Flagler then

1. The Royal Poinciana, Palm Beach, Florida, 1895. 2. The Breakers and Clarendon hotels, Daytona Beach, Florida, 1899. 3 and 4. The Ponce de Leon Hotel, St. Augustine, Florida. 5. The golf course at the Breakers, Palm Beach.

put up a casino and the less expensive Alcazar Hotel opposite the Ponce de Leon; these Moorish structures held shopping arcades, a luxurious indoor swimming pool and tennis courts.

On January 10, 1888, Flagler brought in all his rich friends, who arrived in their private railway cars for a gala opening. "At a given hour on the

appointed day," wrote Florida historians Alfred and Kathryn Hanna, "a cannon boomed, flags were unfurled, the gates of the Ponce de Leon rose slowly, an orchestra struck up 'The Star Spangled Banner' and down the street came a great omnibus drawn by six white horses, bringing guests from the station." The guests approved, Flagler was thrilled, and the new resort became the place where everybody wanted to spend the winter. But the idyll lasted only five years: boredom and the depression of 1893 drove the rich to other pastures and other pursuits. Flagler lost a fortune in this enterprise, but didn't seem to care a great deal. The whole venture cost him a only few months of tax-free oil revenue, and he was in it for the fun as much as the money: when his financial manager advised firing his expensive French chef and New York orchestra, Flagler told him to hire two more chefs and two more orchestras.

While his fellow millionaires licked their wounds, Flagler sped down to Palm Beach on his new railroad tracks. Legend has it that in 1878 the bark Providencia, loaded down with coconuts bound from Havana to

Barcelona, had gone aground there. The locals planted the coconuts around what was then a swampy peninsula bounded on the East by the Atlantic and on the West by Lake Worth. The coconuts became palms, the entrepreneur put up another great hotel, and another fashionable resort blossomed. The Royal Poinciana was begun on May 1, 1893, and opened less than a year later, which gives an idea of the resources Flagler could command. Guests could roll right up to the entrance in their private railroad cars, which were then shunted away to sidings as servants' quarters.

The hotel's dimensions were vast. E-shaped and six stories tall, it was the largest wooden structure in the world. It could sleep 1,750 guests; its gardens, tennis courts and golf courses covered thirty-two acres. Its architectural motif could best be described as shingled Georgian Revival painted yellow with white trimming – like an over-inflated cottage.

The staff were exhausted by walking its corridors. Outside, guests were transported in "Afromobiles": wheeled wicker chairs propelled by black cyclists,

who sat behind so as not to spoil the view. New York's Four Hundred quickly made Palm Beach the winter equivalent of Newport, and in their wake flocked the social hopefuls of the nation. Palm Beach life echoed that of northern sea resorts: the ladies went sea-bathing, covered head to toe in black suits; everybody then dressed for an enormous lunch at the hotel, whose menu read like that of a great ocean

1. "Afromobile" drivers waiting for guests outside the casino and, in the background, the buildings of the second Breakers (built in 1904), Palm Beach, Florida. 2. Gardens of the Boca Raton Hotel and Club (opened as the Cloister Inn in 1926), Boca Raton, Florida. 3. The Royal Palm Hotel founded in 1895, Miami, Florida.

liner. Afternoon was a time for sports or excursions to the nearby jungle, and at tea time everybody changed clothes again and met at the Poinciana's famous Coconut Grove to tango and cakewalk before rushing off to change clothes yet again for dinner and cotillions in the ballroom.

The Poinciana was so successful that Flagler built another great hotel directly opposite: The Palm Beach Inn. Additions were made soon after and the name was changed to "The Breakers", in reference to the Vanderbilt's "cottage" in Newport. The hotels were linked by a horse-pulled bus. For himself Flagler had Carrère and Hastings build the Whitehall for 4,000,000 – more than his entire St. Augustine complex had cost. This was Versailles in the tropics; marble and bronze were used so profusely that it is a miracle the whole structure didn't sink into the bog. Louis XIV, XV, and XVI were intermingled in the reception halls and sixteen guest suites embellished with velvet, silk and satin from Europe's finest shops.

Palm Beach, unlike so many other resorts, has survived. The Poinciana was torn down in 1934, and the Whitehall is now a museum. But the third Breakers (first and second Breakers were destroyed by

fire in 1903 and 1925) still dominates the beach as a marvelous monument to this gilded age; Donald and Ivana Trump carry on Flagler's tradition for mad extravagance in Mar a Lago, formerly the home of Marjorie Merriweather Post.

Meanwhile, Henry Plant was busy on the other coast with two great creations, the Tampa Bay Hotel and what is now the Belleview-Biltmore in Belleair. (He also had palaces in Boca Grande, Punta Gorda and Fort Myers.) The Tampa Bay Hotel must be one of the most eclectic monuments ever conceived: Venetian windows and Moorish gingerbread arches are crowned by onion domes which bring to mind a Russian Orthodox church. One stopped there en route to Cuba by boat. Flagler also had his eye on Cuba, and his last great project was extending his railroad across the Florida Keys to Key West, one of the greatest engineering feats of the time. On the way, Flagler's tracks passed by Miami, where he launched the Royal Palm Hotel in 1896.

Miami's flowering, however, came a bit later with the land boom of the 1920s, and coincided with the rage for "art deco", launched in 1925 at the Paris *Exposition Internationale des Arts décoratifs*. The small hotels of this period are in the older part of town and, happily, are now being restored. The next renaissance of Miami Beach came with the development of the Lapidus hotels discussed earlier.

1. The Grand Plaza, Miami Beach, Florida. 2. A pastry chef of the Whitehall Hotel with his pièce de résistance, Palm Beach, Florida, 1930; in 1926 Flager's residence, the Whitehall, was enlarged with a tower and became a hotel; the tower was demolished in 1959 and the Whitehall turned into a museum. 3. The Breakers, Palm Beach, Florida.

One fundamental difference has grown up between Miami Beach and Palm Beach over the years which should not be overlooked in

a history of American *hotellerie*. The original resorts were pious places for God-fearing Christians, where prayers were as much a part of daily life as mineral baths. Saratoga Springs broke the mold, but non-Christians were never welcome into the better clubs or resort hotels. This gave birth to what was known as "the restricted hotel", to which Jews, no matter how successful or distinguished, were denied entrance. Thus, Palm Beach was a Christian preserve while Miami became a predominantly Jewish resort, a division which still exists although it is not officially admitted. Palm Beach does have its Jewish country club, which is semi-restricted: it has one Christian member.

GLAMOUR IN THE SKY

While Flagler and Plant built up Florida, New

York was developing economically. More hotels went up and, as the action moved uptown, the biggest players were the Astors, whose ancestors had built the old Astor House. Descendants of a butcher from the Bavarian village of Walldorf, they owned vast tracts of New York City, bought long before as farmland. By the end of the nineteenth century, New York's population had grown one hundred and tenfold and the Astors were sitting on a colossal fortune and wonderful hotel sites.

The first Waldorf-Astoria required *two* Astors. William Waldorf Astor built his Waldorf in 1893. This splendid, thirteen-story turreted structure was an immediate success, grossing nearly $5,000,000 its first year. Expansion was clearly in order, but the other half of the block at Fifth Avenue and Thirty-Fourth Street was occupied by the mansion of William's aunt. John Jacob, aunt Caroline's son, agreed to demolish his mother's house and become a partner on condition that his annex be three stories higher and physically separate in case he and cousin Bill had a falling

out. Thus, the Waldorf-Astoria, designed by Henry J. Hardenbergh, was born. Its grand galleries like the famous Peacock Alley, the legendary maître d'hôtel Oscar, and

the Waldorf Salad exemplified a rarely parallelled way of life. The entrance on 33rd Street was embellished like the most glorious Italian palazzo; that on 34th Street, with its great marble-columned porte cochère was reminiscent of St. Petersburg's Winter Palace. There was a Turkish Salon with silver armour where tea was served by a genuine Turk and his boy assistant, a Great Ballroom in white and gold and a sitting room that looked like the Uffizi. The private dining rooms were copies of those in the Astor mansions and filled with the usual cornucopia of European furniture, textiles and carpets. A brilliant manager, George Boldt, emulated César Ritz and made the hotel a center for all sorts of social and intellectual functions, and his excellent dining rooms quickly attracted the customers of the popular

Delmonico's and Louis Sherry restaurants. For the first time in the

1. The Breakers, Palm Beach, Florida. 2. The Waldorf (1893), New York City. 3. The Waldorf's main entrance, on 33rd Street, New York City, 1893. 4. The St Regis, New York City; inaugurated in 1904, this establishment was designed as an apartment hotel; but it has functioned as a traveler's hotel ever since it opened.

history of New York a hotel became the center of the city's brilliant social life. And the Waldorf Men's Cafe – the Bull n' Bear – was where J.-P. Morgan, Henry Clay Frick and other titans met to cut deals after the close of the stock exchange. This Waldorf-Astoria's days came to an end after only three decades of existence: in 1929 it was demolished to make way for the Empire State Building.

Not long after the Waldorf-Astoria was built, John Jacob commissioned the St. Regis, at eighteen floors then the city's tallest hotel. « Colonel » Astor, a scientific dabbler, introduced extraordinary modern advances, among them a thermostat in every room and a central vacuum system. The St. Regis, at 55th Street and Fifth Avenue, has been one of the glories

of New York. Its great bronze revolving doors and marble floors have greeted pleasure-seekers going up to debutante parties in the roof's pink ballroom or heading down to the Russian nightclub run by Prince Serge Obolensky, a razor-thin aristocratic Astor-in-law. And, during his winter residence there, Salvador Dali received his friends in state on a large armchair in the hall with his pet ocelots on a leash.

The very year the St. Regis was built, three businessmen met there for lunch and decided to knock down the Plaza Hotel. They had just bought it for $3,000,000 but, doubtless inspired by the St. Regis's splendor, they felt that their eight-story pile of brick and brownstone was no longer up to the

standards of the day, even though it was among the most beloved and best-run hotels in the city. They hired Henry J. Hardenbergh, the Waldorf-Astoria's architect, and Fred Sterry, the manager of the Royal Poinciana and the Breakers. Thus were born the new Plaza's Palm Court, embellished by four caryatids from an Italian baroque palace; the dark-paneled Oak Room, which looked as if it had been removed intact from an Imperial German ocean liner; and the wonderful Edwardian Room, filled with light and looking out onto Central Park and a dream-like vision of horse carriages clopping along West 59th Street. The endless gilded salons, ballrooms and large suites are still the playground for Eloise, that naughty girl who so fully personifies the thrill of being spoiled in a grand hotel. The Plaza, is, of course, a stopping-off place for businessmen from all over the world. Most of all, however, its is one of the middle-class New Yorker's favorite Sunday distractions, where gypsy violins and palm trees reward a week's struggle in the asphalt jungle. And now, after years of serving as a link in a chain of less-distinguished hotels, it is being carefully renovated by its new owners, the Trumps.

The Waldorf-Astoria, St. Regis and Plaza all belong to an age that was to be blown apart by World War I. In its wake came Prohibition, which radically changed hotel life. There wasn't much point in meeting in great public rooms and restaurants to drink mineral water. Bootleg liquor was happily imbibed in bedrooms and

1. The old Plaza, New York City, about 1896 ; originally built in 1888, the old Plaza was replaced by the present-day building in 1907. 2. The Plaza in 1907, New York City. 3. Menus from the new Waldorf-Astoria, New York City. 4. The Commodore Hotel, built in 1919, New York City.

suites instead. Prohibition nevertheless caused serious financial damage, and many hotels went under. But the United States had taken on new prestige with World War I, and the large ocean liners were now packed with visiting Europeans; they all landed in Manhattan needing hotel rooms. Also, as the city grew larger and more uncomfortable, the rich moved to Connecticut and Long Island, and needed a pied-à-terre in the city. Between Prohibition and the

Depression, there was a crescendo of building activity in both transient and residential hotels. Classical hotels included the 500-room Ambassador (1921), whose sober facade occupied a whole block on Park Avenue, and the 1,100-room Roosevelt (1924), the first New York Hotel to include ground-floor shops.

And, naturally, hotels developed around train stations, although the English terminal-hotel never caught on. Grand Central had its Biltmore, whose clock rang bells for the first trysts of generations of college kids who met beneath it, and Pennsylvania Station had the Governor Clinton Hotel (1929) and the New Yorker (1930), whose 2,503 guest rooms are now filled by the followers of the Rev. Sun Myung Moon, who owns it. As residence hotels, Park Avenue had the Drake, Barclay and Park Lane, all built between 1924 and 1927. On side streets were the Dorset, Lombardy and Lowell, and on Lexington Avenue the 1,200-room Shelton. Holding its crown high above the crowd is the splendid Ritz Tower. Designed by Emery Roth, known for his tall and elegant twin-spired apartment houses livening up the Central Park West skyline, the Ritz is a masterpiece of art deco

skyscraper design. The gracious tower, springing from a broad base, houses exquisite duplex apartments.

But the grandest hotel of all was on the way, surging ahead on a sea of eternal optimism – although the contract for the $ 42,000,000 new Waldorf-Astoria was signed on Black Thursday, to the sound of stock speculators' bodies hitting the

sidewalk. The new Waldorf-Astoria, designed by the firm of Schultze and Weaver, is one of the best remaining examples of large-scale art deco architecture in America. Its limestone twin towers looking down over Park Avenue create a profile that epitomizes the romance of New York in the thirties, the ideal setting for a Fred Astaire and Ginger Rogers movie.

Architectural historian Paul Goldberger wrote that the 1930 version of the Waldorf presented "a dazzling array of ballrooms and shops, nightclubs and restaurants, more varied activity than any single skyscraper had ever contained. Suddenly it seemed that the whole

1. The Roosevelt Hotel (built in 1924), New York City. 2. The Drake, New York City. 3. The chapel in the Biltmore Hotel, New York City ; the Biltmore was one of the few American hotels with a built-in place of worship. 4. The Caswell-Massey shop in the Hotel Barclay, New York City, 1956.

world – or at least the world of fantasy – could be contained in a single tower."

The beauty of its art deco paneling and ornamentation, the sophistication of its stucco decoration, the splendid marble main lobby with its  silver urns raised above the Park Avenue entrance, have been splendidly preserved for more than half a century. The finest decorators in New York and Paris designed the suites and public rooms, in an unlimited variety of styles. The Sert Room; the Empire Room, where so many wonderful entertainers have performed; the three-story-high ballroom for 6,000 guests; the new Peacock Alley and monumental main hall are a synthesis of the taste of the time. In the history of style, the Waldorf-Astoria is the equivalent of the Normandie oceanliner – a showcase of the very best a nation could produce.

It is also a repository of history. The Waldorf Towers, a separate section with its own entrance on 50th Street, welcomes nearly every visiting head of state; it is always used by Presidents of the United States and is the home of America's Ambassador of the United Nations. For many years it housed Douglas McArthur, the Duke and Duchess of Windsor, Cole Porter, Adlai Stevenson and giants of industry, commerce and finance. Today, its heavily-carpeted suites host United Nations General Assembly delegations from around the world.

Twenty thousand people attended the Hotel's opening, many arriving in the usual private railroad cars, for which a special siding had been created directly below the hotel. President Hoover delivered the opening address: "I have faith that, in another fifty years, the growth of America in wealth, science and art will necessitate the institution's moving to an even more magnificent place." America has grown, but no finer hotel has been built within its frontiers.

A TALE OF TWO CITIES

The capital of the United States is by no means one of its largest cities. Washington, D.C. reflects the dignity of the nation through Pierre L'Enfant's street plan and the classically inspired monuments lining its wide boulevards. Washington is curiously European considering its national purpose, and it simultaneously brings to mind Berlin's old Wilhelmstrasse, London's Whitehall and Paris's Avenue Matignon. Its many embassies lend a cosmopolitan touch, and dignified public buildings make clear that its business is government. The glamour of the capital is manifest in the White House and the State Department, in the grandeur of ambas-  sadorial residences and in Georgetown's private mansions. Despite steady streams of tourists and visitors doing business with the government, Washington has not been distinguished by grand hotels until relatively recently. In the mid-nineteenth century, the National was the only decent one in town.

The first truly world-class hotel was the Arlington (1868) opposite the White House, to which it was practically an annex during the McKinley and Theodore Roosevelt administrations. The Willard, between the Capitol and the White House on Pennsylvania Avenue, dominated the hotel scene as of 1901. Built on the site of an earlier Willard, this large Beaux-Arts structure by Henry J. Hardenbergh fell into disrepair after World War II; it has just

1. An advertisement for the Ritz Tower, New York City, 1930. 2. The Prince and Princess of Monaco at the Waldorf-Astoria during the 1950s, New York City. 3. The 'new' Willard followed a hotel with the same name which was built in 1850. Washington, D.C.

recently been restored. It is the Mayflower, however, that comes to mind as the quintessential Washington hotel. It was designed by Warren and Wetmore, the same firm that designed Grand Central Station in New York City. Ten stories high, the majestic cream-colored palace was finished in 1925. The Mayflower was a second home to Harry Truman, who breakfasted there regularly when President, as well as to the FBI's J. Edgar Hoover, who was always to be found at the same table at lunchtime. Had he lunched at the Watergate, history might have changed.

The most American of cities is neither Washington nor New York. It is Chicago, which lies at the epicenter of the country's heartland and looks neither East nor West. Built on Lake Michigan, enriched by farmlands as well as industry, Chicago sets the tone for Middle America. It was at the forefront of the skyscraper revolution, as well as the nation's busiest railroad hub. After the Civil War, Chicago grew in size and importance as the East and West coasts were united by rail.

One used to enter Chicago through the giant stockyards that received most of the country's livestock for slaughter. Union Stockyard opened in 1865 and soon processed 6,000,000 hogs and 3,000,000 head of cattle a year. One cow that wasn't slaughtered belonged to Mrs O'Leary, and on October 8, 1871, legend says, it kicked a lantern into a bale of hay and started a fire that destroyed 18,000 buildings and left 90,000 homeless in a city of 300,000 inhabitants. Among the buildings destroyed were all of Chicago's hotels, including two of its most famous – the

1. *The Palmer House dining room, Chicago, Illinois. 2. The 'Gold Coast Room' in the Drake Hotel, Chicago, Illinois. 3. The Jefferson Hotel, Chicago, Illinois.*

"fireproof" Palmer House and the Grand Pacific, which had just opened. With them went the Tremont and Briggs House, the finest of older hotels.

For Potter Palmer, a successful dry-goods merchant and cotton speculator, hotels were just one of many ventures. He was a pivotal figure in the development of downtown Chicago and was also responsible for the rise of the Gold Coast on Lake Shore Drive, where his wife Bertha ruled local society from a turreted castle. Palmer also built his partner Marshall Field's splendid retail store, a Beaux-Arts masterpiece in a city filled with splendid buildings. In 1870 he opened the first Palmer House, near Field's store, and soon began a new hotel on State Street. Palmer was in a rush to open before the new Grand Pacific, but the true race started after the Great Fire, since Palmer House I and II, as well as

the competition, had been destroyed. Palmer worked night and day on what might be called Palmer House III, great searchlights illuminating the work in progress. He ran second but built the better hotel.

Palmer had studied the great palaces, and he was able to import superior building materials duty-free due to an Act of Congress passed to relieve fire victims. His eight-story hotel contained 700 rooms and was the first hostelry with electric lights and a telephone in each room. Its richly ornamented facade rose from giant storefront windows, which lent an extraordinary sensation of lightness. The hotel surpassed everything previously built in Chicago and is fondly remembered for its barber shop, whose checkerboard tile floor was whimsically inlaid with two hundred and twenty-five silver dollars. The competing Grand Pacific followed many of the same design principles but was not as well proportioned.

The Great Fire opened the floodgates for a wave of real estate speculation unprecedented in American history. The building boom spawned numerous apartment houses influenced by new concepts in hotel design. Many had public dining rooms and parlors, and great architects like Louis Sullivan were involved in their conception.

The boom also resulted in a plethora of hotels that were perhaps larger, but far less grand than their magnificent predecessors. The first new skyscraper hotel was the Blackstone (opened in 1908) which rapidly became a center of social life. It is always difficult to reconstruct the original interiors of hotels because of redecoration, but the Blackstone's exterior survives: all the wonderful Beaux-Arts ornamentation of the Palmer House and Grand Pacific seems to have been pushed up to the roof. The Blackstone inspired other behemoths that served the swell of commercial travelers,

1. The Congress Hotel, Chicago, Illinois.
2. A wedding reception at the Blackstone, Chicago, Illinois. 3 and 4. Dustin Hoffman, and Humphrey Bogart and Lauren Bacall at the Ambassador East Hotel, Chicago, Illinois.

transit passengers from the trains and, in later years, conventioneers.

The convention is a particularly American rite, and Chicago is the convention center of America. These gatherings of common interests or trades are often only excuses for a vacation, and without conventions American hotels would go bankrupt. Every summer, Chicago gathers up red-fezzed Shriners to its warm bosom, and tens of thousands of Masonic Lodgers walk the hot pavements waving flags and shuttling from hotel to hotel in buses to drink and make merry. A bus tour of Chicago with them is the perfect way to make the rounds of the hotels which sprang up between the wars. One good way to start exploring would be with a bright and cheery lunch at the Drake Hotel. Rubbing elbows with the taller skyscrapers on either side of it, standing on the banks of Lake Michigan, the Drake was inaugurated in 1920. Its architect, Ben Marshall, entered the field relatively late in life, after already having made a name for himself in fashion. The Drake's architecture still testifies to Marshall's

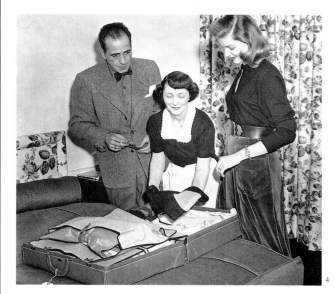

vivid imagination. A recommended next stop is the Chicago Hilton and Towers, known as the Stevens Hotel when its doors first opened in 1927. At that time it was hailed as the biggest hotel in the world. Last but not least, the visitor who feels like basking in one of the most elegant atmospheres

in the city should wrap up a tour by exchanging a few toasts in the Ambassador East's famous Pump Room, a gathering place for stars of the political and show business worlds for half a century.

THE NOT SO WILD WEST

It is appropriate that George Pullman built his luxury carriages just south of Chicago, the center of America's railroads. The life of hotels is intimately linked to transportation and Pullman set a standard of comfort that rapidly spread to Europe, Russia and Asia with the *Compagnie Internationale des Wagons Lits.* His railways cars, as comfortable as the hotels his passengers visited, opened a new era of travel. Until the plane took over after World War II, the most luxurious way to cross the country was to take the Twentieth Century Limited to Chicago, stop for lunch the next day at the Ambassador East's Pump Room, and proceed on the Super Chief to Los Angeles. From the moment one stepped from Grand Central Station's red-carpeted platform into a sleek, stainless-steel Pullman until arrival in Los Angeles three days later, time flew by in a delicious routine of dinner in the diner, card-games, drinks in the lounge car, changing landscape, visits by Fred Harvey's salesmen with Indian jewellery of

turquoise and silver in velvet-lined carrying cases, and occasional stops such as Santa Fe, New Mexico, where real Indians hawked pottery and rugs that would probably be museum pieces today.

The West was opened when the railroads replaced the stagecoach. We all have visions of pioneers hammering a golden spike into the rails that finally crossed the great divide, of whooping Indians on horseback chasing trains filled with terrified ladies in crinolines. The West is a great dream, a place of promise and pleasure, a magnet drawing visitors from the entire planet to its unparalleled natural wonders: great deserts, salt lakes, sulphurous geysers, giant redwoods, the Grand Canyon and the national parks at Yellowstone and Yosemite. Ancient adobe villages and deserted mining towns bear witness to the West's past, and nowhere is the air so clear or the light so bright.

Many hotels have been built to exploit these gifts. The Rocky Mountains dominate the West and have given birth to several splendid resorts, the most important being Colorado Springs, South of Denver. The first hotel to go up there was the Antlers in 1882, named for the profusion of horns embellishing

1. The Majestic Hotel (inaugurated in January 1927), Hot Springs National Park, Arkansas. 2. The Capital Hotel, Little Rock, Arkansas. 3. The Old Faithful Inn, Yellowstone National Park, Wyoming. 4. The fire which destroyed the Arlington, April 5, 1923, Hot Springs National Park, Arkansas.

its lobby. The first Antlers was a pleasant country inn in Queen Anne style, with shades of Saxony and Holland. It boasted good plumbing and ventilation and – like so many other hotels – went up in smoke.

It was replaced in 1901 by a fantastic palace hotel plucked from Montecatini with Renaissance loggias, shaded balconies and incredibly luxurious private and public rooms of the quality of a great English country house. It was torn down in 1964, but the Broadmoor still thrives in the same resort. Designed by Warren and Wetmore and built in 1918, this nine-story pink palace had a great marble staircase, a Georgian ballroom with the usual crystal chandeliers, a golf course, bridle paths, polo fields, squash courts and

tennis courts indoor and out. Those seeking nature could drive to Pike's Peak and visit the hotel's Cheyenne Mountain Zoo on the way.

Other excellent hot springs resorts were the Montezuma Hotel in Las Vegas Hot Springs, New Mexico (1882) and the Hotel Colorado in Glenwood Springs (1893), which had a two-story bathhouse and a swimming pool five hundred feet long, the largest hot mineral bath in the world. Soaking, however, was not the object in the West any more than it was in the East. It was the great national parks that drew people, and the grand hotels met the needs of the most demanding customers. At the Grand Canyon they could stay at the El Tovar (1901), built on top of the canyon a mile above the Colorado River. The views were spectacular; it wasn't even necessary to

venture outdoors. It had the moose heads, Indian carpets and wicker furniture of a mountain retreat and all the modern comforts of a palace. In Yellowstone Park were two excellent hotels, the Old Faithful Inn (1902-1903) and the larger and more spec-

tacular Canyon Hotel (1910-1911). They were both made of natural materials – stone bases, timber and shingles – and they blended beautifully into the landscape. The giant living room of the Old Faithful had a stone fireplace rising through three floors of ornamental log staircases and balustrades; except for the rows of rocking chairs it would have been the perfect setting for Act I of Wagner's *Die Walküre*, in which the unsuspecting Siegmund falls into his enemy Hunding's hall. The Canyon Hotel, more pretentious and more comfortable, was inspired by Frank Lloyd Wright's Prairie designs. A more perfect expression of Wright's idea was the Arizona Biltmore, designed by Albert McArthur, who had trained at Wright's studio in Oak Park, Illinois. The lobby, a two-hundred-and fifty-foot perspective of lintels of molded and sculpted concrete blocks, marries modernism and the Toltec temple.

The most elegant lodging in the national parks, however, is the Ahwahnee, in California's Yosemite Valley, opened in 1927. This splendid six-story structure is set against soaring mountains, and it was decorated by two scholars, Phyllis Ackerman and the renowed Islamicist Arthur Upham Pope; their efforts compensate for the lack of air-conditioning. The art of the

1. Opening day speech given by President Roosevelt on September 28, 1937, at the Timberline Lodge, Mount Hood, Oregon. 2. Entrance of the Canyon Hotel, Yellowstone National Park, Wyoming. 3 and 4. Decorative detail and facade of the Timberline Lodge, where the outdoor scenes of the Stanley Kubrick film 'The Shining' were shot.

Southern Indians influenced the fabrics and murals, but America's early dwellers had never known such extravagance.

MEET ME AT THE PALACE HOTEL

Yosemite Valley is but one of California's many wonders. The state's extraordinary quota of sunshine, rich farmland, deep forests, beautiful beaches, deserts and mountains draws young and old in search of an easier and more natural environment. California is as much a way of life as it is a place. It was gold, however, not sunshine, that beckoned the first great wave of immigrants. Until 1846, California was a distant outpost of the Mexican Empire and San Francisco a dusty village of four hundred inhabitants. It was in 1848 that a man digging a ditch near Sacramento found gold in the common clay; less than a year later

shiploads of fortune seekers – the famous 49ers – were pouring into San Francisco and heading for the hills. By 1850 the city's population was 25,000 , of which ninety percent were men. They needed lodging when they returned to town, their pockets filled with nuggets and gold dust, and the first hotels were quickly thrown up. So desperate was the need that the ships in the harbor, abandoned by the dozen by their gold-seeking crews, were hauled ashore and used as rooming houses. Wooden shacks housed miners fifty to a room; they paid heavily for the privilege. A

flea-ridden bunk cost $30 a week when an excellent hotel in New York or Boston charged $2.50 a night.

Several years later the town became more civilized, and by 1880 it was a delicious mixture of Victorian gingerbread houses, excellent restaurants, theaters, a stock exchange and an opera house that drew Europe's finest singers. It also had a magnificent hotel, appropriately called the Palace, as well as other first-class hotels: the Cosmopolitan (1859), the Occidental (1861), the Russ House (1862) and the Grand (1869).

The Palace was conceived and financed by William C. Ralston, head of the Bank of California. He spent $5,000,000 to create the largest and most magnificent hotel in America at that time. It covered an entire city block; each of its 755 bedrooms was 20 feet square. It had all the usual large public rooms filled with massive furniture, but its most famous feature was the Grand Central Court, one hundred and forty-four feet long by forty-eight feet wide. Paved in marble and filled with tropical plants, statues and fountains, it was the site of concerts every afternoon, and at night it was illuminated by more than 500 multicolored gas lights. The hotel was supposed to be impervious to the

earthquakes that always threatened the region, and with twelve-foot-thick foundation walls, it seemed built for eternity. So did the St. Francis (1904), and the Fairmont (1906) on Nob Hill, that aerie of such plutocrats as Huntington, Stanford and Crocker.

1. The Palace Hotel, San Francisco. California. 2. A chorus in front of the St. Francis, San Francisco, California. 3. The Fairmont Hotel, San Francisco, California, 1907. 4. Dan London, one of the managers of the St. Francis, in front of photographs of celebrities who have stayed in the hotel. 5. The Mark Hopkins, San Francisco, California.

The St. Francis was built with Crocker money by Henry Scott and Charles Green, guardians of the grandchildren of the patriarch Charles Crocker. Architects and hoteliers were sent around the world to seek inspiration. Returning home in 1901 they declared, "Whatever is best in the Ritz establishments (the hotels of César Ritz) we shall adopt. All our china and silverware will be patterned after the Carlton designs and the coloring and general decoration will also be from the Ritz hotels." Grand marble columns topped with gilded Corinthian capitals set the tone in the lobby of this great place. The 450 guest rooms were perfect Victorian parlors: plush and brocade, with dark mahogany furniture and a telephone – then a rare luxury.

The telephone was of little use on the morning of April 18, 1906, when the entire city seemed to heave into the air. James Hopper, a journalist who lived opposite the hotel, wrote that "the St. Francis was waving to and fro with a swing as violent and exaggerated as a tree in a tempest." Three-foot waves of earth rolled through the landfill areas of the city. Enrico Caruso, jolted awake in the Palace, clung to his bed and had to be pried loose by his manager. He and other members of the Metropolitan Opera then fled to safer ground – the St. Francis which was still intact, if shaken. John Barrymore, the renowned Shakespearean actor, felt secure enough to return to his room, leaving Caruso

to his breakfast downstairs.

The great earthquake was just the start of the disaster. Gas mains broke and flames rapidly devoured the wooden houses when water mains broke as well, crippling the fire department. A wall of smoke and flame enveloped the city; by nightfall two square miles of downtown had been destroyed.

Here, as in Chicago, rebuilding began in short order. Julia Morgan, who would become America's pre-eminent woman architect and perhaps the finest architect in California, redesigned the Fairmont, with its lovely Laurel Court and elegant lobby in white, gold and marble. It opened in 1907, as did the restored St. Francis, with a new wing. Several other new hotels were built, and on December 15, 1909, the beloved Palace reopened, signalling the close of the San Francisco's reconstruction.

In time, other establishments followed this first generation of hotels and, rivalling their illustrious predecessors, themselves became nothing less than institutions. During the Great Depression the Sir Francis Drake, which Conrad Hilton acquired in 1937, momentarily eclipsed the St. Francis. The Fairmont also went through some rough times during the Thirties, and ended up being bought by the owners of the 20-story Mark

1. Entrance of the Mark Hopkins, San Francisco, California. 2. A banquet in honor of the Shah of Iran, St.Francis Hotel, San Francisco, California, 1954. 3. Tents pitched in front of the Fairmont Hotel after the 1906 San Francisco earthquake. 4. The Claremont Hotel, Berkeley, California.

Hopkins, a handsome neo-gothic landmark decorated with delicate terra cotta motifs. It was the talk of the town when it opened in 1926. But international fame didn't come until 1939, when the private apartments on its twentieth floor were converted into a bar lounge offering a spectacular panoramic view of the city. The "Top of the Mark" is the only place in San Francisco where diners are treated to a sweeping vista of the entire city and its hills, the surrounding mountains, the bay on one side and the ocean coastline on the other, the majestic Golden Gate and Bay Bridges, and the Pacific stretching into infinity. Those old enough to remember still reminisce about the wives and fiancées of departing GIs who used to gather at the Top of the Mark during World WarII and, bidding one last farewell, watched the troop ships sail off beyond the horizon.

HOLLYWOOD DREAM

Visitors have been attracted to southern California since the railroads linked San Diego to the rest of the country in 1885, and some of the resorts that sprang up became small cities. Among the earliest was Coronado Island opposite San Diego's harbor. The Hotel del Coronado was the West's answer to the Ponce de Leone in St. Augustine. Completed in 1888, and then reached only by ferry, this large, turreted, white-shingled structure embellished with entertaining red conical towers and lace-like balconies, sheltered an interior open court planted with exotic flowers and shrubs among which frolicked monkeys and tropical birds. For the less glamorous and less rich, the hotel put up a tent city, and for all there was a race track, boating facilities and an ostrich farm as well as rodeos, concerts and parades. Other fine resort hotels rose along the entire coast, from the Mexican frontier near San Diego to Vancouver in the north. Among the finest was the Biltmore in Santa Barbara, built as a private beach-front estate in the early 1900s and opened as a hotel

in 1926. But the most original was the Mission Inn (1903) at Riverside, which had, among other wonders, a Spanish baronial music room with a soaring carved ceiling.

Today the beauties of the coast are too often spoiled by urban development, but until World War II even Beverly Hills was more resort than city while downtown Los Angeles and Hollywood were centers of the great movie studios. Freeways and skyscrapers have made a city of this once-bucolic village in which film personalities carried on while the world

breathlessly watched; until recently, there was even a bridle path down the center of Sunset Boulevard. The stars lived on and around Sunset, but their lives were planned at that legendary pink palace, the Beverly Hills Hotel. This hotel, built in 1912 by Burton Green, has always been the focal point of the celluloid world. Deals are made in suites off palm-patterned corridors, in the Polo Bar's darkness, or in the sunlight reflected from the pool, whose cabanas are alloted according to status. The separate bungalows have long been the scene of scandalous affairs that would eventually be sniffed out by Louella Parsons or Hedda Hopper and broadcast around the world.

Driving a few miles along Sunset Boulevard, one enters the elegant iron gates of the Bel-Air, a patrolled

residential property for the stars of the moment, complete with a small golf course and the Bel-Air Hotel (1941). It has lodged generations of film stars in town to complete a film, as has the Beverly Wilshire (1928) in downtown Beverly Hills. Built in the spanish Mission style, the Wilshire has now been

1. The Mark Hopkins Hotel, San Francisco, California. 2 and 4. The Biltmore Hotel. Santa Barbara, California. 3. Hotel del Coronado, San Diego, California. 5. The Beverly Hills Hotel pool, Los Angeles, California.

totally renovated, with duplex suites named for great French fashion designers and champagnes, and a marble Louis XV ballroom. The truly historic ballroom is downtown at the much larger Biltmore. It was here that the Academy of Motion Picture Arts and Sciences was founded and the first sketches of Oscar scribbled on a linen tablecloth.

But on the whole, Southern California lacks exciting hotels. The film people they were built to serve were almost excessively easy to please. Many of those who went West to invent the Movies had been poor immigrants or immigrants' children from New York's Lower East Side. The starlets were often farmer's daughters chasing dreams, and many a cowboy hero had really been living on the range only a few weeks before arriving in the City of dreams. To them, any hotel was better than a bunkhouse, any bed better than a bedroll.

East or West, then, each coast built according to its own sources of inspiration. New York, welcoming the great and titled of Europe, naturally drew on the Old World. The West, on the other hand, was settled by immigrants not from Europe but from America's crowded, urban East. In Hollywood, some of these same pionneers improvised a strange and wonderful new industry.

But East or West, Hollywood's unique mixture of cheerful frivolity, creative invention, and seriousness of purpose is akin to the spirit of American hotel building. The technical achievements, grandeur, and sense of fantasy found in American grand hotels are paralleled in many an Oscar-winning production. And, like Hollywood's innovators, the flair, daring and imagination of their builders have been part of the American dream.

NEW
YORK
—and the—
NORTHEAST

Boston's Tremont introduced the modern concept of the "Grand Hotel", but it was soon eclipsed by new establishments. One of the most famous, the Parker House, opened in 1856; it had enough rooms and lounges to make sure that a hundred "gentlemen" were comfortable. Like many of its contemporaries, the Parker was visited only by men, who used it as a club. It was a favorite meeting place for intellectuals, in much the same way that other establishments welcomed politicians or professionals in addition to their transient guests. Many of New England's great enlightened minds could be found conversing brilliantly around the Parker House's table on a Saturday night: Oliver Holmes, Ralph Waldo Emerson, Louis Agassiz. The mood was elegant, though a bit austere, and the American grand hotel of the 1860s was already taking on its social role. ≈ Above: the Parker House was rebuilt in 1927; some of the old hotel's furniture was reused, and one of the suites was redecorated to look as it did when Charles Dickens supposedly stayed in it; here, actors pose in the "Dickens bedroom" in May, 1927. Inset, left, the old Parker House. Opposite, right, the wing added in 1884. Right page: the Vendome Hotel, built between 1870 and 1880. Preceding pages: the Sherry-Netherland and Savoy Plaza, New York, 1930s.

Boston's Statler and Ritz-Carlton were both inaugurated in 1927. Two establishments, two styles: one was typically American, the other very much influenced by Europe. The Statler capped the already-rich career of E.M. Statler, who imposed his own standards of comfort and luxury when he created a major hotel chain. Ten years earlier, this brilliant innovator had the then-revolutionary idea of installing a bath tub in every room; at the Statler of Boston he added a radio. For the first time in the United States, hotel guests could listen to their favorite programs in their rooms rather than in the lounges. The Ritz-Carlton's management, on the other hand, relied on the seductive charm and atmosphere of "old Europe": the hotel boasted bouquets of freshly cut flowers, cosy fires crackling in the fireplaces, restaurant service on every floor, and elevators which were perfumed every day. ≈ Above: the Statler's main lobby, around 1930, and facade; the hotel has been rechristened the "Boston Park Plaza". Opposite: a brochure listing the Statler chain's services, 1930s. Right page: the Ritz-Carlton's opening day dinner on May 17, 1927, and the cover of a menu for a special occasion.

Ritz-Carlton Hotel
BOSTON
MASSACHUSETTS

"Here I am in New York. The Fifth Avenue Hotel, where I am staying, merits a few words. In Europe this type of establishment is unimaginable. Here, everything is at your fingertips. Everything except a polyglot: don't even bother looking for a single French-speaking employee among the 200 working here. On the other hand, what charm, what amenities! For twenty dollars you obtain a room, a salon, and the right to eat all day long. Meals are taken in a dining room on the first floor. At the entrance to this immense gallery, a hearty maitre d'hotel comes up to you and shows you to your table. Don't try to resist, don't insist on one spot or another; you have to give in, those are the rules." From Jacques Offenbach's travel notes during his American tour, 1876. ≈ Above: the Fifth Avenue Hotel in 1899, and the hotel's facade in 1874. Opposite: the lobby; the Fifth Avenue was torn down in 1908. Right page: the Chelsea Hotel around 1900; this apartment building, converted into a hotel in 1905, would go on to be a favorite place of residence for writers.

"It's clear that, other than the service, everything you hear about the comfort and elegance of American hotels is underestimated. These colossal houses envelopping as many as 1,500 rooms have often been described; their wealth and luxury, their huge dining rooms, their lounges and lobbys have been praised many times. Whether it's the Netherland or the Astor, the St. Regis or the Imperial, or so many others whose names escape me, all of them are magnificently appointed with marble, stucco, bronze, gold, silk drapes, brocaded hangings, paintings by Bouguereau, and vases by Tiffany." C. Huard, *New York comme je l'ai vu*, 1906. ≈ Opposite, from left to right: a lounge in the Ritz-Carlton in 1911; the Tea Room in the Prince George Hotel in 1905; the library in the Biltmore, 1913; a room in the Marie Antoinette (Broadway and 66th St.), 1896; a turn-of-the-century view of New York; the Playroom reserved for guests' children in the Biltmore, 1913; the Palm Room in the St. Regis, 1904; a suite in the Vanderbilt, 1917; the Endicott's lobby, 1908. Below: the Hotel McAlpin and Hotel Pennsylvania.

At nightfall, the dark mass of the Astor Hotel looked as if it were crowned by lights. The brightly-illuminated balcony on the top floor set off the green copper roof; at the top of the building, hanging gardens radiated the sparkling glimmer given off by countless lamps and chandeliers up towards the sky. This heavenly nightime vision was a typical New York scene: since the 1880s, parties and other leisure activities had been moved up to the city's rooftops. The tradition originated with the theatres. Before air-conditioning existed, New York's theatres were forced to close down during the city's infernal summer heat waves. But in 1882 the Casino Theatre had the idea of opening an outdoor theatre on the building's roof. Little by little, urban dwellers got used to enjoying themselves above the city streets; they could keep cool and admire their city from these high altitude palm courts, flower-bedecked cafes, and dance floors. At the Astor Hotel, glasshouses and winter gardens were added, and the roof was open all year round. ≈ Above: the Astor's hanging gardens and, the facade; torn down in the 1960s, this hotel, designed by the architects Clinton and Russel, was built on Broadway at Times Square in 1904. Below: an illustration of the hotel for a brand of cigars, 1910; the Astor was considered a rival of the Waldorf-Astoria. Right page: a car show in the Astor's main lobby, 1914.

The Waldorf-Astoria was the first of a new breed of hotels, both because of the sophisticated services it offered and because of the way the building itself was integrated into the city's social life. Until the Waldorf-Astoria came along, hotels were not considered appropriate places for high society to meet. Giving a dinner or ball in one of them was as inconceivable as entertaining in a train station. But in 1906, less than a decade after the new hotel opened, and at the same time that Henry James wrote *The American Scene,* the Waldorf-Astoria was setting the tone, dictated social etiquette, and had become the favorite rendez-vous for New York's super-rich. James commented, "Here was a social order in positively stable equilibrium. Here was a world whose relation to its form and medium was practically imperturbable; here was a conception of publicity as the vital medium organized with the authority with which the American genius for organization, put on its mettle, alone could organize it. The whole thing remains for me... a gorgeous golden blur, a paradise peopled with unmistakable American shapes, yet in which, the general and the particular, the organized and the extemporized, the element of ingenuous joy below and consummate management above, melted together and left one uncertain which of them one was, at a given turn of the maze, most admiring." ≈ Above: the stately Peacock Alley, where members of high society strolled and flaunted. Inset: Mrs Bradley Martin, who gave a fabulous costume ball in the Waldorf's Grand Ballroom on February 10, 1897. Opposite, right: the Bull'n' Bear Bar, also known as the "Men's Bar." Left page: the Waldorf-Astoria's facade in the 1920s.

When Mrs. Bradley Martin planned her costume ball, she wanted to make sure that no one had ever seen anything like it. It was the first event of its kind to be held in a hotel. The Waldorf's Grand Ballroom, swimming in a sea of flowers, was transformed into a replica of Versailles' Great Hall of Mirrors. Garlands of orchids flowed along the moldings and the mirrors were draped with roses. Blue satin hangings with bouquets of flowers pinned to them rippled in enormous waves across the ceiling. Mrs. Bradley Martin came dressed as Mary Queen of Scots and wore a fabulous diamond cluster that supposedly had belonged to King Louis XIV of France. She greeted other members of New York's upper crust from a gilded dais. ≈ Above: a banquet honoring the King of Prussia in the Grand Ballroom, 1902. Below: menus from gala dinners. Right page: Mrs. Calvin Brice in a Worth dress copied from a Velasquez painting which she wore for Mrs. Bradley Martin's ball.

"We all went in a cab to the old Waldorf-Astoria... on Fifth Avenue, where the Empire State Building now stands. The foyer and the many rooms which led off from it, decorated in early Victorian, were overcrowded, overpowering. There were sofas and chairs resplendent in red plush velvet. Tapestries hung on the walls. Wherever you looked you saw classical statues holding electric light fixtures... The old Waldorf must have been magnificent in its day; but in the summer of 1917 it had the quality of a flower pressed too long between the pages of a book... Could it have spoken to us I am sure it would have said, 'Youth, be wary. Don't look at me with such disdain; I, too, have had my day." Gloria Vanderbilt and Thelma Lady Furness, *Double Exposure, a Twin Autobiography*, 1958. ≈ Below and opposite: two bottles dating from 1907, discovered during demolition of the old Waldorf in 1929; carting away the lamps.

T he statutes for the new Waldorf-Astoria were signed on the same day as the stock market crash in 1929. That did not keep Lucius Boomer, who also headed the old Waldorf, from immediately contacting the architectural firm of Schultze and Weaver. Boomer did not leave the master builders much time for thought; it was a Thursday and he wanted the plans on his desk by ten o'clock on the following Monday morning. That was a tall order even for Schultze and Weaver, who had already graced the New York City

skyline with the Sherry-Netherland and the Pierre. The firm hired the best collaborators they could find, paid them staggering sums, and on Monday morning submitted a design of the facade as well as the interior from the ballroom to the barber shop. Since Prohibition was still in effect, the only thing missing was the bars. But Schultze and Weaver's plan was so well thought out that the hotel facades required almost no changes. ≈ Above: the main lobby. In 1931 the gold-veined marble was quarried especially for the Waldorf-Astoria. Inset: a detail of the elevator doors leading to the ballroom. Opposite, left: the old and new Waldorf-Astorias. Right page: frescoes from the lobby facing Park Avenue.

"I've been waiting a long time in the scented, over-heated lobby of the Plaza; so long, in fact, that I am starting to wonder if anything's gone wrong. Suddenly I realize that I am in the Savoy-Plaza: my rendez-vous was across the street. Tired and confused, I sit down at the bar in the Plaza: fortunately, the person I was supposed to meet is still waiting for me there. The Martini livens me up. I watch the people. I am surprised at the women. They wore flower beds and aviaries in their carefully done up hair." Simone de Beauvoir, *L'Amérique au jour le jour*, 1948. ≈ Women were subject to all sorts of restrictions in American hotels for a long time. Shortly before the second Plaza opened in 1907, the Waldorf-Astoria raised quite a stir by announcing that "ladies" could visit its restaurants at any time of the day. It was up to the maître d'hôtel to discreetly eject women who failed to conform to "respectable" norms of behavior. The Astor followed suit, but its dining rooms remained reserved for women hotel guests only. The Plaza was the most liberal of all: the Tea Room and restaurant let in unaccompanied women with no restrictions at all. However, they were barred from the hotel's Fifth Avenue Cafe until 1920, and the Oak Room remained an all-male bastion until 1950. Below: Eloise, an illustrated children's book character thought up by Kay Thompson in 1948; the adventures of this little girl who lived in the Plaza are part of the hotel's legend. Opposite: some of the Plaza's guests: 1 - Tea time in the Palm Court, around 1940; 2 - Alicia Markova and Douglas Fairbanks; 3 - The portrait of Eloise; 4 - Adele Astaire; 5 - Mrs. Cornelius Vanderbilt and Conrad Hilton; 6 - Mr. and Mrs. Burton; 7 - A debutante ball. Inset: the Plaza's monogram. Preceding pages: a turn of the century scene with the facade of the Plaza on the right.

"The business luncheon took place at the Plaza, a high class hotel with an old fashioned style, a fine style. I like these vast, beautiful hotels which have nothing 'modern' about them but have acquired a past thanks to their rich decoration. There are living pasts and dead pasts. The Plaza reflects a past of simple, monied times." Le Corbusier, *Quand les cathédrales étaient blanches*, 1937. ≈ <u>Opposite</u>: the Plaza's entrance. <u>Above</u>: the Oak Room, which today is one of the Plaza's most famous restaurants, was originally a bar; paneled in dark oak, furnished with leather armchairs, for a long time it was considered the headquarters for bankers and financiers. In the hallways adjoining the Oak Room, New York stock brokers installed offices which were reputed to be the most luxurious in the entire city. <u>Opposite, right</u>: the wine cellar. <u>Inset</u>: Palm Court waitress. <u>Right page</u>: the ballroom.

The Barclay opened without fanfare on November 4, 1926. There were neither official speeches, nor Hollywood stars; the hotel's management wanted to avoid flashy publicity. The reason: the Barclay did not seek to attract passing tourists in search of a room. It was designed to be a sumptuous "apartment hotel", where New York's very rich could take up residence for at least part of the year. The new establishment was promoted in the most natural way possible: all it took was skimming through "Who's Who" or the "New York Social Register" to find that dozens of "excellent families" had selected the Barclay as their home away from home. But the hotel's success would have been incomplete without a representative of the prestigious Vanderbilt family; luckily, Harold S. Vanderbilt was one of its first tenants. He lived in a 17-room penthouse apartment which included a squash court and private gym on the roof. ≈ Above and left page: the Barclay's entrance and a room in one of its suites, 1926. Opposite: Numbering rooms and room service at the Barclay, rebaptised the "Hotel Intercontinental New York" during the 1970s.

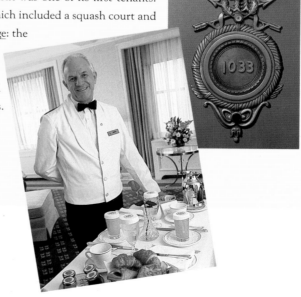

Charles Pierre's Park Avenue restaurant was the "in" place for New York's upper crust during the 1920s. It owed its fine reputation as much to the cooking as to the thoughtful, charming welcome guests received. After a late-night supper, the management made sure that all young ladies were accompanied home. In 1930, Pierre opened what would become one of the world's finest hotels: the Pierre. At this Fifth Avenue establishment, guests enjoyed both the inimitable service Pierre was famous for and – as might be expected – excellent food. ≈ Above: Auguste Escoffier and his staff on opening day: October 1, 1930. Right: the present-day chef at the Pierre. Opposite: views of the 61st St. entrance hall. Preceding pages: a bellhop from the New Yorker hotel demonstrating his craft to students in hotel management, 1930.

There are no huge lobbies at the Pierre, but rather the quiet, intimate atmosphere of a fine hotel in London or Paris. This beautiful building, which looks like a skyscraper version of a French chateau, has been a bastion of European elegance in New York City since 1930. In fact, the Pierre's odyssey began in Europe, where Charles Pierre was born. Starting out as a bell-hop at the Hotel des Anglais in Monte Carlo, he quickly found out how extravagant the demands of the princes, archdukes, and false archduchesses who visited the Riviera at the time could be. A stay in Paris taught him the secrets of French cuisine; then he met Louis Sherry during a visit to London. That's when he decided to "conquer" America. In New York Sherry ran a restaurant which bore his name and rivaled Delmonico's. He hired Pierre in 1904. The 12 year-long partnership ended because of a timely debate: high-society women had grown used to smoking in public, and a scandalized Sherry decided to ban them from his restaurant. Pierre respected his clientele's sight to enjoy themselves and resigned. He soon opened his own restaurant. Fittingly enough, it was his flair at hospitality that eventually let him build the Hotel Pierre: the project's backers were among his most loyal clients and fervent admirers. But the tumult of the 1930s did not spare the hotel, and it went bankrupt in 1932. A bitterly disappointed Charles Pierre died soon afterwards. Paul Getty bought the Pierre in 1938, and to this day the hotel has pursued the tradition of hospitality made legendary by its founder. ≈ Above and opposite right: the reception desks in the 61st St. entrance hall. Inset: the Fifth Avenue entrance in the 1930s. Right page: breakfast at the Pierre.

Even the most sought after resorts go out of style. Wealthy New Yorkers no longer frequented Manhattan Beach and Coney Island, when they became enormous amusement parks in the 1890s. The well-to-do would also desert the Catskills and Saratoga Springs when establishments there could no longer offer them all the modern comforts. ≈ Above and opposite: the veranda and an advertisement for the United States Hotel, Saratoga Springs. Below: a reception room in the United States Hotel. Left page: the Grand View Hotel, probably built in the 1870s, Coney Island, Brooklyn.

Around 1890, Atlantic City's star began to rise as the fortunes of Long Branch and Cape May went into a decline. The elegant ambience that reigned in these first seaside resorts was gone forever: the beachfront palaces rebuilt after the 1902 fire catered mainly to the nouveaux riches. On Sundays, factory workers from Philadelphia and rich businessman rubbed elbows on the boardwalk. During the 1920s Atlantic City was at the pinnacle of its popularity; not even thirty years later it, too, sank into near-ruin. The Traymore and Marlborough-Blenheim Hotels had become cumbersome white elephants and were demolished during the 1970s. But gambling was legalized in 1976 to revitalize the forlorn resort. Since casinos were allowed only in hotels, a few of the old relics managed to escape the architectural massacre. ≈ Above: reception lounge and advertisement for the Ritz-Carlton. Opposite: a hallway in the Ambassador Hotel. Below: the Dennis, Marlborough-Blenheim, and Traymore Hotels. Right page: the Traymore and the Breakers. Background: demolition of the Old President Hotel, 1979.

Philadelphia had a head start in the race to become the most important city in America. Site of the signature of the Declaration of Independence, considered by many to be "the cradle of the nation", it was the capital of the United States from 1790 to 1800. But its prestige declined during the nineteenth century, when it was overtaken by Boston and New York. The advent of the Civil War stimulated economic activity in Philadelphia, which provided Union troops with equipment and supplies. Changes in the hotel landscape reflected this return to prosperity. The old American House, the Girard House, or the La Pierre Hotel, all built between 1844 and 1854, couldn't rival the Continental Hotel, opened in 1860, on Chestnut Street, in the middle of the business district. It had the city's finest jewelers and art dealers for neighbors. The hotel contained a shopping center and a huge hall called the "Business Exchange", which was exclusively reserved for financial dealings. The Continental alone witnessed as many business transactions as did all of Chestnut Street's importers and retailers. ≈ <u>Above</u>: the Continental Hotel's entrance lobby, around 1860; and the facade of the Arcade Hotel, also built on Chestnut Street, but which did not manage to survive after the Continental came along. <u>Opposite, right</u>: the Continental's "business Exchange". <u>Right page</u>: the Walton, which opened in 1896 and was torn down in 1966.

"The most comfortable of all the hotels of which I had an experience in the United States, and they were not a few, is Barnum's, in that city (Baltimore); where the English traveller will find curtains to his bed for the first and probably the last time in America, and where he will be likely to have enough water for washing himself, which is not at all a common case." Charles Dickens, *American Notes*, 1842. ≈ The venerable port city of Baltimore was endowed with some remarkable hotels from very early on. Barnum's, open from 1826 to 1889, was one of the most prestigious. Later the Rennert, well known as the local stronghold of the Democratic Party and today likewise gone, was acclaimed for the abundance and excellence of its food. Its oyster bar was the most celebrated in the whole city: the waiters had become real experts at the art of shucking shellfish and joking with customers, which created a jovial mood and, naturally, earned them handsome tips. ≈ Above and right page: lounges in the Rennert, around 1910; founded in 1885, this hotel was torn down in 1941. Opposite: Barnum's facade.

By the turn of the century, the Rennert, which remained Baltimore's only "grand hotel", no longer matched contemporary standards of elegance and modernity. Its parties and cheerful atmosphere had gone out of style and high society was looking for more sophisticated ways to enjoy itself. A new hotel was built on the site of an old estate named "Belvidere": the name of the future establishment was ready-made. But the management couldn't decide whether it should be called "Belvedere" or "Belvidere"; consulting the *Century Dictionary* was no help, since it suggested both spellings. Finally, after a seemingly endless debate the "Belvedere" Hotel was christened in 1903. The plans were drawn up by the Boston architectural firm of Parker and Thomas, who, just back from a long stay in France, designed an edifice which was powerfully influenced by the Beaux-Arts style. When it opened, the Belvedere was considered the last word in chic and comfort. Only people listed in the local social register were allowed into some of its lounges; that way, ladies who had their tea at the hotel would not have to fear for their reputations. One frequent visitor was a young woman named Wallis Warfield, who lived nearby. Nibbling on petits fours in the hotel, little could

she imagine that years later a king would give up his throne for her and that she would be known as the Duchess of Windsor. ≈ Above: the Belvedere's bar, 1915. Opposite: two ladies in afternoon gowns leaving the hotel after tea time, 1918. Below: an advertisement from the 1910s. Right page, from left to right: the tea room and the main dining room; the ballroom; the billard room and barber shop, 1908. The Belvedere is still open for business.

There's a saying that the second-best address in Washington, D.C. is the Mayflower Hotel – the best being the White House, of course. Even this ranking was once under reconsideration ; President Truman openly preferred the Mayflower. Since it was founded in 1925, the Mayflower has actually served as an annex of the Presidential mansion, even taking on semi-official functions: the great ball celebrating the election of a new president takes place at the Mayflower; foreign dignitaries visiting Washington are put up in this hotel; the first mainland Chinese delegation to the United States stayed there for eight months while its new embassy was being set up. Sometimes the Mayflower's management even untangles touchy situations that otherwise would have turned into diplomatic incidents. When Nikita Khrushchev visited in 1959, President Eisenhower requested that the White House's gold table service be used. But when Khrushchev wanted to organize a dinner at the Soviet embassy to return the invitation, he was faced with the embarrassing problem of having to find a gold service himself. The Mayflower came to the rescue! Golden plates dishes, and cutlery left the hotel's vault for the embassy, where the evening turned out to be a great success. The Mayflower's maître d'hôtel received an enormous jar of beluga caviar as a token of thanks. ≈ Inset: the Mayflower's facade. Below, from left to right: Mamie Eisenhower at a birthday party given by the Women's National Press Club, 1953; a statue in the hotel; President Harry S. Truman having breakfast, 1950. Left page: the Mayflower's main entrance on Connecticut Avenue, 1928.

Famous Mayflower guests: 1 - General de Gaulle arriving at the hotel in 1945; 2 - Clare Booth Luce and Walt Disney chatting in the lobby; 3 - Jacqueline Kennedy, Walter Seligman (the Mayflower's banquet director), and Roger Stevens (the first director of the Kennedy Center for the Performing Arts), 1962; 4 - A U.S.O. dance during World War Two; 5 - For nearly forty years, F.B.I. director J. Edgar Hoover ordered the same lunch and sat at the same table; here he is with an aide, Mr. Tolson; 6 - Actor Brian Aherne boosting wartime moral, around 1942; 7 - Mrs. Richard Nixon greeting guests at a party in 1953; 8 - Margaret Truman and Missouri Senator Stuart Symington during a banquet, 1954; 9 - "Big Mac", the Mayflower's biggest guest, who took part in an information campaign organized by Western cattle breeders, 1972. Below: Burton Caynor who was the Mayflower's head bellhop, 1933.

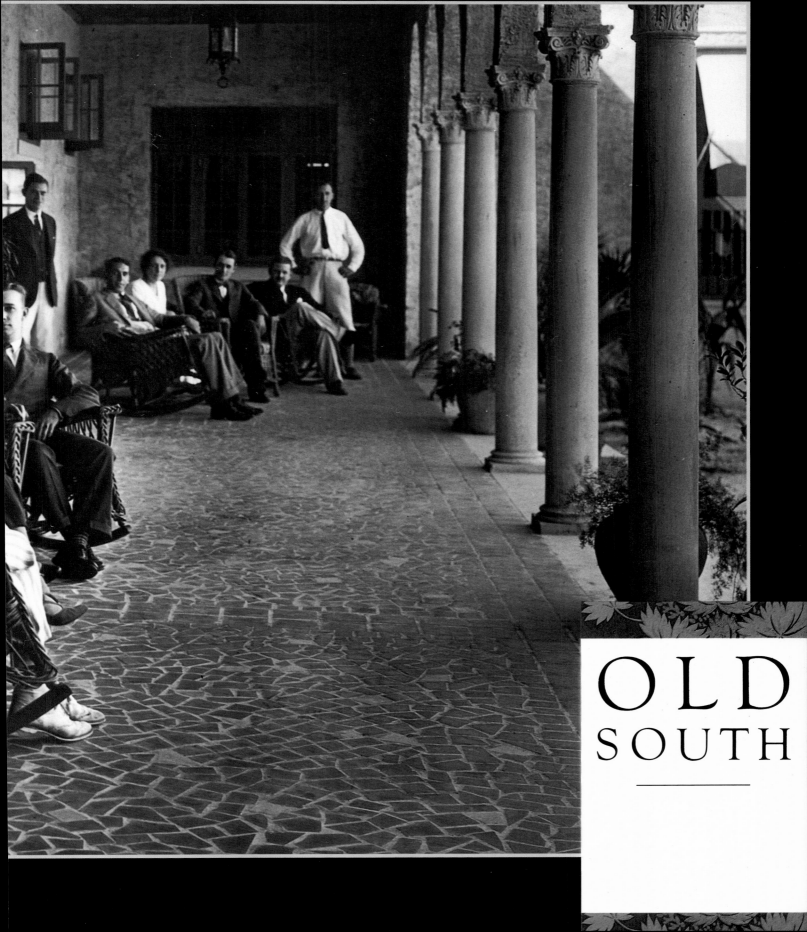

OLD
SOUTH

Travelers looking for a vestige of the special atmosphere that characterized the "Old South" have a chance of finding it at the Greenbrier. Its graceful portico of dazzling whiteness is reminiscent of the genteel antebellum plantation mansion. But the Greenbrier was built in 1910, well after the South's Golden Age had come to an end. It was constructed to complete White Sulphur Springs' first hot springs resort hotel, the Grand Central, better known as "Old White", and erected in 1858. The Greenbrier's outstanding success has led to constant expansions since opening day. It continued to be profitable even during the Great Depression. While many hotels were closing down after the 1929 stock market crash, the Greenbrier was more prosperous than ever: local families found it cheaper to spend a season at the hotel than pay the upkeep on their own estates. ≈ Above: the Greenbrier's pool, around 1920. Below: the lounge where guests "took the waters". Right page: an advertisement from the 1930s and, inset, the winter garden and the hotel's facade. Preceding pages: the veranda of the Casa Loma Hotel, Coral Gables, 1920s.

FOUNTAIN IN SPRING ROOM, THE GREENBRIER, WHITE SULPHUR SPRINGS, W. VA.   1A-H34

The Greenbrier
and Cottages
White Sulphur Springs
West Virginia

America's
Most Beautiful
All-Year
Resort

Winter Leases

L. R. JOHNSTON, General Manager

Legend has it that the marble staircase adorning the Jefferson Hotel's central lobby served as the model for the famous flight of steps up which Rhett Butler carried Scarlett O'Hara and down which she later fell in rage. Whether this story, is true or not the hotel would have made a wonderful set for *Gone With the Wind*. Designed by the same architects who did the Ponce de Leon Hotel in St. Augustine and built in 1895, it survived two serious fires. Declared a historic landmark in 1969, the Jefferson-Sheraton was restored in 1986; only the alligators who once picturesquely paddled around the hotel's decorative ponds and wandered around in the hallways are missing. ≈ Above: the Jefferson Hotel's facade and rotunda in 1895. Opposite: the facade after the 1901 fire and an advertising brochure. Right page: the statue of Thomas Jefferson underneath the Jefferson Sheraton's restored skylight.

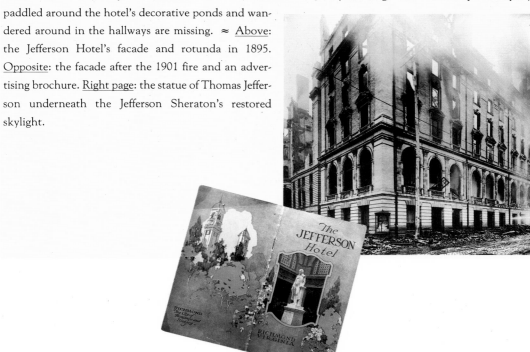

According to a legend, an Indian brave was bringing a message to a tribe on the Atlantic shore when he stopped, exhausted, on the banks of a hot water pool for a rest. He took a drink and suddenly felt like a new man. He had just discovered Hot Springs, where the first hotel was built in 1766. But the resort didn't really take off until 1832, when the first elements that would eventually give rise to the renowned hotel complex known simply as "The Homestead" were constructed. ≈ Below: the Homestead's entrance portico and gardens as seen from the dining room, around 1930. Opposite: bath house, the Homestead, around 1890.

In December 1860, South Carolina became the first state to secede from the Union. The decision was made at a national convention in Charleston. For the next five years, life in this and so many other peaceful and refined Southern cities would be shattered by civil war. Hotels in the upper-class part of town, like Mills House (built in 1853) or the Charleston Hotel (founded in 1839) were turned into headquarters for the Confederate armies or havens for rich landowners who had fled their planta-tions. ≈ Above: Mills House in happier days, before the war. Right page: the same hotel, still standing after the fire that devastated the city in 1861; General Robert E. Lee watched the disaster from the hotel's first floor balcony. Below: Recruiting volunteers in front of the Charleston Hotel in February 1861.

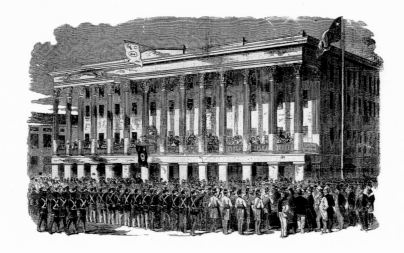

Louisville had two grand hotels in the nineteenth century: the Louisville, constructed in 1835, and Galt House, founded in 1838 and rebuilt in 1869. Although Galt House had the reputation of being one of the finest hotels in the United States, Charles Dickens, who stayed there, didn't mention it at all when he wrote his *American Notes*. He had a good reason: when the hotel manager, a certain Major Throckmorton, came into his room to welcome him and find out if there was anything he needed, Dickens showed him out and replied irascibly, "When I need you, landlord, I'll ring for you!" The major, who didn't appreciate Dickens' testy attitude, simply had his illustrious guest expelled from the premises. ≈ Above: the Louisville Hotel (which would be demolished in 1940). Opposite: menu from a banquet in honor of Grand Duke Alexis, Galt House, 1872. Right page, above: the menu used by Galt House during the weeks following President Garfield's assassination, 1881; below: menu for a banquet organized by a group of British residents for Queen Victoria's birthday, Galt House, 1883. Galt House was torn down in 1920.

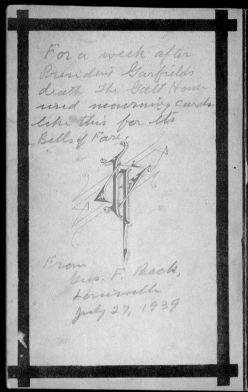

For a week after
President Garfield's
death The Galt House
used mourning cards
like this for its
Bills of Fare.

From
Geo. F. Beck,
Louisville
July 27, 1939

1881, Sept. 25

GALT HOUSE

D. J. SPRAGUE.

1883, May 24

Banquet
in honor of the
Sixty-fourth Birthday
of her Majesty
Queen Victoria
BY
THE BRITISH RESIDENTS
OF LOUISVILLE, KY.
U.S.A.

AT THE
GALT HOUSE
MAY 24TH 1883.

"She had a debut after the armistice, and in February she was presumably engaged to a man from New Orleans. In June she married Tom Buchanan of Chicago, with more pomp and circumstance than Louisville had ever known before. He came down with a hundred people in four private cars, and hired a whole floor of the Muhlbach Hotel." F. Scott Fitzgerald, *The Great Gatsby*, 1925. ≈ Fitzgerald's "Muhlbach Hotel" was inspired by the Seelbach, built in 1907. The Seelbach flourished during the 1920s, taking on the role that Galt House had held during the previous century. ≈ <u>Below</u>: the Seelbach's bar, 1920s and 1940s. <u>Opposite</u>: one of the rooms in the recently-restored Seelbach.

"The Mississippi Delta begins with the lobby of the Peabody Hotel and ends in Catfish Row in Vicksburg. The Peabody is the Paris Ritz, the Cairo Shepheard's, the London Savoy of this section. If you stand near its fountain in the middle of the lobby, where ducks waddle and turtles drowse, ultimately you will see everybody who is anybody in the Delta..." Historian David Cohn, 1935. ≈ The first Peabody Hotel, built in 1869, was a sophisticated establishment that boasted seventy-five rooms and a ballroom. Getting to it, however, meant crossing some of Memphis' darkest, most unsavoury streets. Buggies hitched to uncooperative mules regularly got bogged down in mud, and the Peabody's guests arrived worn out and splattered after pushing their carriages to the hotel door themselves. Nevertheless, the local elite faithfully kept coming to the Peabody. In 1925, it was replaced by the building still standing today. In 1930, one of the hotel's managers got the idea of putting ducks in the Peabody's lobby foutain. Twice a day ever since, a red carpet leading to the fountain is been rolled out and, to the accompaniment of music, the famous ducks make their way to the artifical pond waiting just for them. ≈ Left page: an evening's end at the Peabody.

Constructed in New Orleans in 1835, the first St. Charles Hotel was a real architectural triumph. Towering over the city's other buildings and crowned by a dazzling white dome, it could be seen from just about anywhere. An 1845 guide boasted that "even the stoical Indian and the cold and strange backwoodsman, when they first view it, are struck with wonder and delight." The gorgeous hotel went up in smoke and flames in 1851, but a second St. Charles rose from the ashes. Visitors relished its ultra-modern comfort: the bathrooms had hot and cold running water. Another fire destroyed the St. Charles in 1894, but its successor didn't leave anyone awestruck this time: America had gotten used to luxury hotels. ≈ Inset: the silverware at the first St. Charles. Below: a la carte menu of the second St. Charles, 1857. Opposite, left: a view of the third St. Charles (the red building), which would fall to the wrecker's ball in 1974.

L ocated in New Orleans' French Quarter, the St. Louis was built at the same time as the St. Charles. The local creole aristocracy strove to preserve a certain image of France and of "le chic parisien" by giving lavish parties and receptions behind a facade patterned after the Rue de Rivoli in Paris. But the most notable space in the St. Louis was the "Rotunda", the site of daily auctions where anything could be bought or sold, including property, art, and slaves. Harriet Beecher-Stowe portrayed the sale of Uncle Tom and his plantation companions in a hotel which was similar to the St. Louis in every respect. After the Civil War the St. Louis – renamed the Royal – became run-down. ≈ Above: the Grand Staircase in the St.Louis; below, right: paintings and slaves being auctioned in the "Rotunda". Inset: the Hotel Denechaud, built in the French Quarter in 1906 and later successively renamed the Hotel De Soto and the Pavillon Hotel.
Right page: the Denechaud's bar and dining room, 1906.

In the nineteenth century, the citizens of New Orleans flocked to balls, the theatre, the opera and the Mardi Gras carnival was becoming an institution. When jazz was born all America was throbbing to the beat of this city which looks upon partying as a serious art. More than anywhere else, hotels were at the heart of having a good time. Residents claim that one of America's first night clubs was born in the Grunewald, a hotel built in 1893. Located in the cellar of the Grunewald, this place was unique: artificial waterfalls cascaded down its walls and stone-carved faces peered out at diners from a forest of stalactites. Many of the day's most famous vaudeville stars performed at the club, and by 1900 it was the hotel's main attraction. Rebuilt in 1908, the Grunewald became the Roosevelt Hotel in 1925. A dozen years later, a new night club opened: the Roosevelt's Blue Room. The best jazz musicians played in an incredible setting: from 1938 to 1940 the room was turned into a desert oasis planted with palm trees. The ceiling was studded with stars that blinked on and off with clouds that came and went. Sometimes it even rained! ≈ <u>Above</u>: the main lobby of the Roosevelt (renamed the Fairmont in 1967) and, <u>inset</u>, the hotel entrance. <u>Opposite</u>: the kitchens and the chefs. <u>Left page</u>: the Blue Room and the hotel's porters in the 1940s; <u>inset</u>, a matchbook cover advertising the hotel.

Vacationing in Florida: 1 - A picnic on the boardwalk of the Palm Beach Bath and Tennis Club, 1927; 2 - arriving at the Casa Loma Hotel, Coral Gables, 1925; 3 - the veranda of the Vinoy Park Hotel, St. Petersburg, about 1925; 4 - the Alcazar Hotel, St. Augustine; 5 - the "Venetian" pier at the Cloister Inn (renamed the Boca Raton Hotel and Club in 1930), Boca Raton, 1926; 6 - the Miami Biltmore Hotel, Coral Gables, 1926; 7 - the Casa Loma's orchestra, Coral Gable, 1925; 8 - tea dance at the Flamingo Hotel, Miami Beach, 1920s; 9 - the Alcazar Hotel's pool, St. Augustine. Below: an advertissement for the Miami-Biltmore Hotel in Coral Gables; and a tourist brochure boasting Miami's charms, 1920s.

2

3

6

8

9

"You had to be financially more or less at your ease to enjoy the privileges of the Royal Poinciana at all; enjoy them through their extended range of saloons and galleries, fields of high publicity all; pursue them from dining-halls, to music rooms, to ball-rooms, to card-rooms, to writing-rooms, to a succession of places of convenience and refreshment, not the least characteristic of which, no doubt, was the terrace appointed to mid-morning and mid-afternoon drinks – drinks, at the latter hour, that appeared, oddly, never to comprise tea, the only one appreciated in 'Europe' at that time of day." Henry James, *The American Scene*, 1907. ≈ Above: an afternoon concert in the Royal Poinciana's celebrated Coconut Grove, 1904; and a birds-eye view of the enormous hotel. Below: an advertising brochure, 1928. Right page: the Royal Poinciana's veranda, 1904. Following pages: the Breakers' "Grande Loggia" (today named the "Mediterranean Ballroom"), Palm Beach, 1926.

At first, nothing hinted at the fabulous destiny in store for the place the Indians called "Mayami", which means "Inland lake". In 1890, the village settlers had named Miami consisted of 1,500 inhabitants huddled around a post office, trading post, and what was left of a fort that had been hastily built during the war against the Seminoles. Just ten years later, it was proclaimed "America's sun porch". The undistinguished area blossomed into a city in 1897 thanks to the efforts of Henry Flagler who, with his rival Henry Plant, had already been largely responsible for turn-

ing Florida into a favorite tourist destination. He decided Miami's fate by building a rail link to Palm Beach and erecting the Royal Palm Hotel, which opened on January 16, 1897. Designed by the same architects who had done the Royal Poinciana, this new hotel was a smaller version of the Palm Beach palace and boasted all of its features: a graceful wooden structure laid out around either side of a central body, and a facade painted a striking lemon-yellow. On the 290-foot long veranda or in the observatory perched atop the six-story rotunda, the hotel's guests turned into ardent admirers of Miami. Though the Royal Palm was torn down in 1930, a number of splendid Art Deco hotels built around the same time are its worthy successors; visitors can still bask in their rocking chairs on sunny porches and terraces all along this famous beach. ≃ Above: the Royal Palm's pool, around 1900. Insets : a swimmer, the circular six-hole golf, and the Royal Palm's facade.

Once a small, sleepy town, Saint Augustine was transformed into a resort as soon as the Ponce de Leon opened on January 10, 1888. The local paper hailed the event: "Saint Augustine is launched on a new era as one of the most magnificent resort towns in these United States. Prominent men and their families from all parts of the country have come to Florida for the first time to be present on this auspicious occasion, for at last, thanks to the efforts of Henry M. Flagler, Florida is no longer a "frontier" state but promises to be the new-found playland of America." Indeed, the Ponce de Leon, which signaled the start of Flagler's hotel empire, made winter vacationing in Florida fashionable. But unfortunately, Saint Augustine didn't get as much out of the southward rush as it had hoped. It had grown too fast and, more important, was poorly served by railway lines. Flagler added the Hotels Alcazar and Cordova in 1889, but the Ponce de Leon's glory faded quickly. Nowadays, Saint Augustine, the oldest town in the United States, is sprucing up its picturesque image. The Alcazar now houses a museum and the Ponce de Leon is host to Flagler College.
≃ Above: the Ponce de Leon's facade and dining room. Below: a lounge and, right page, the hotel's rotunda. Following pages: the Hollywood Beach Hotel, Hollywood, Florida.

The facade of the Don CeSar Hotel, built in 1928, on the beach at Pass-A-Grill (today part of St. Petersburg). After taking on successive roles as a fashionable hotel palace, an Air Force convalescent center, and an office building, the Don CeSar was abandoned in 1969. Vandalized, covered with graffiti, and threatened with demolition, it was saved at the last minute in 1972 and reopened to the public in 1973.

Wood was used in hotel construction in Florida perhaps longer than in other parts of the country. Henry Flagler and Henry Plant, who had used brick and even concrete for their palaces in St.Augustine and Tampa, suddenly reverted to wood to erect their last hotels. It made sense to use pine, which was plentiful in Florida and had the reputation of hardening with age. But apparently a craze for the French colonial style, whose skillful woodwork was so well-suited to resort hotel architecture, also determined this choice. Wooden palaces sprung up all over the state during the 1890s. It's not surprising, alas, that this was also the Golden Age of hotel fires and the first two Palm Beach Breackers burned to the ground. When Henry Plant backed the construction of the Belleview in Belleair (which opened in 1897), it was feared that it would suffer the same fate. But nothing of the kind happened. Considered "the largest occupied wooden structure in the world" to this day, the Belleview managed to stay untouched by fire. To preserve this precious relic for good, its facade was covered with the newest type of aluminum siding, coated with a plastic finish which is treated to perfectly simulate grained wood clapboards. ≃ Above and opposite: the facade of the Belleviev, renamed the Belleview Biltmore in 1919. Right Page: the veranda.

CHICAGO
—and the—
GREAT
PLAINS

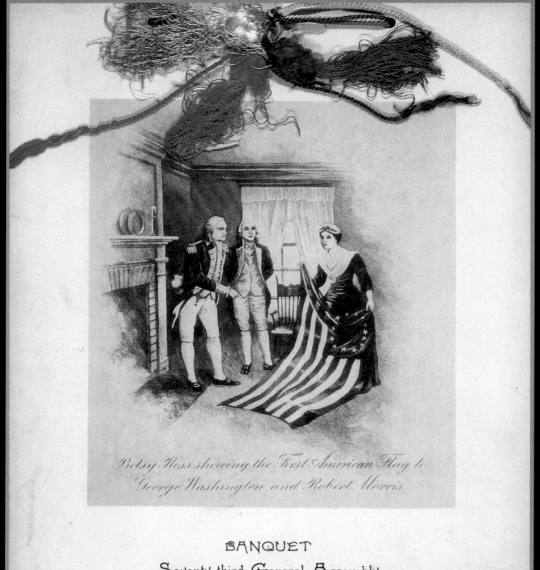

Betsy Ross showing the First American Flag to George Washington and Robert Morris

BANQUET

Seventy-third General Assembly

◎ 1899 ◎

HOTEL DESHLER
Columbus, Ohio
Louis C. Wallick   Adrian L. Wallick

Great Southern Hotel & Theatre, Columbus, Ohio.

The late 19th century was a period of growth for the state of Ohio. Agriculture and industry were booming, factories were humming away and smokestacks filled the skylines of major cities. Naturally enough, there was a growing demand for well-equipped hotels designed to provide visiting businessmen with all the modern comforts. One such establishment was the Chittenden, built in the state capital, Columbus, in 1895. The hotel was the site of conventions and committee meetings of all kinds. Business was conducted in the conference rooms and dining rooms alike; travelling salesmen could meet clients and sign contracts without ever leaving the hotel — even to relax: when it opened, the hotel had two theaters within its walls. The rival Great Southern, which opened in 1896, went one step further and boasted a grand "Opera House" in addition to its other attractions. ≈ Above: the Great Southern Hotel and Theater. Opposite: the Chittenden. Left page, top: menu from the Great Southern's dining room, 1899; bottom: the Deshler, built in Columbus in 1916. Preceding pages: ball held at the Drake in Chicago, 1950.

J.S. Buckingham, an English visitor to St. Louis in 1840, described that city's nine hotels as being among the worst he had ever seen: "Even the best of them, the National Hotel, is greatly inferior to the second and third-rate hotels of the Eastern cities." A year later St. Louis boasted a new hotel, the Planters, financed by two Bostonians, and as big and elegant as the famous Tremont House. St. Louis needed new hotels, for the city was growing rapidly thanks to its expanding port facilities and its strategic location on the road to the West. As in Ohio, most visitors were "passing through"; they were often in a hurry and more interested in bodily comfort than in opulent surroundings. Indeed, Missouri hotels would be among the first to offer guests certain modern conveniences. The Victorian Hotel built in 1888 in Kansas City, for example, was the first to equip each of its rooms with a bath — this would not become common practice in the rest of the country until much later, when the Statler chain made it one of their policies (see page 42). ≈ <u>Above and opposite:</u> interiors and facade of the Jefferson, another famous hotel in St. Louis. <u>Right page:</u> the Lennox lobby, St. Louis, 1920.

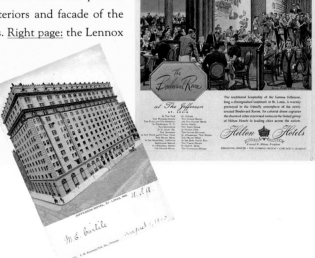

The « old » Palmer House, built just after the great Chicago fire, was still the finest hotel in town in the early years of the twentieth century. By the 1920's, however, its age was showing ; it was in need of a face lift and lacked many modern comforts. In 1925 it was replaced by the current building designed by Holabird and Roche. Though the new hotel, with its 2268 rooms, never achieved the reputation of its predecessor, it was doubtless one of the most elegant buildings of its day. The interior decoration was particularly well conceived and refined. The main lobby, for example, was decorated with murals attributed to Louis Pierre Rigal, who, several years later was to work on the newly-built Waldorf-Astoria in New York. According to documents in the hotel's archives, these murals were painted in France, shipped to Chicago in 1926 and placed on the ceiling of the main lobby where they remain to this day. ≈ Above: entrance to the Empire Room and view of the main lobby. Below and left page: portions of the murals that decorate the ceiling of the main lobby.

Palmer House's spacious Empire Room, now used mainly for Sunday brunches, banquets and receptions, is famous. Opened to the public during the Chicago World's Fair in May of 1933, the room was decorated in the Empire Style, an evocation of the splendor of the Napoleonic era. The gold, the dark green panelling and wall hangings, the gilded effigies of the Emperor and Josephine all contribute to the creation of a particularly French atmosphere. A rather hurried remodeling in 1945 led to the temporary disappearance of the splendid chandeliers that Potter Palmer had imported from Europe; they had been sold to an antique dealer for $ 400 each. Five years later the hotel management, regretting their sale, repurchased them at the then going price of $ 4000 a piece! ≈ Above: dinner-shows held in the Empire Room were a major attraction until 1972; this photograph was taken during a Maurice Chevalier show. Inset: facade of the original Palmer House, 1873. Below: pictures from a brochure announcing the opening of the «new» Palmer House in 1925. Right page: the original Palmer House had one floor entirely reserved for women guests; pictured is a woman staying in those quarters around 1880.

"Yes, Chicago had charms. 'Some day', I told Mary, 'I'm going to come back and find a vacant lot. I'd like to build me a hotel here.' I didn't know that someone, right that minute, was saving me the trouble; had found the vacant lot and was putting up the Stevens, the largest hotel in the world. It would be twenty years before I embarked on the adventure of buying the Stevens. And it was quite an adventure." Conrad Hilton, *Be My Guest*, 1957. ≈ When it opened in 1927, the Stevens was not only the biggest hotel in the world but also the most costly to build. Never had a great international hotel been so expensive – amounting to the tidy sum of 30 million dollars, only the new Waldorf Astoria would cost more. For years, Conrad Hilton had been eyeing the Stevens. Finally, in the first years of the Great Depression, when many grand hotels were being sold at bargain prices, Hilton felt the time had come to buy. But the Stevens was not for sale. It would not become part of the Hilton chain until 1945. In 1951 it was renamed the "Conrad Hilton"; finally, in 1985, it became the "Chicago Hilton and Towers." ≈ <u>Above</u>: the Stevens family, who created the Stevens Hotel, 1927. <u>Inset</u>: a drawing room in the Chicago Hilton and Towers. <u>Opposite</u>: children's playroom in the Stevens, around 1930. <u>Right page, top</u>, the ballroom around 1950; <u>below,</u> President Kennedy visiting the Conrad Hilton.

" **A**s in so many Grand Hotels in the U.S., you can find everything at the Blackstone Hotel: stamps, postcards, a post office, telegraph service, theater tickets, movie tickets, radios, a bank, books, ties, razors, lighters, toothbrushes and even *Le Figaro*. The elevators at the Blackstone shoot you up like catapults and are as luxurious as drawing rooms in the Primavera style.» Paul Achard, *Un œil neuf sur l'Amerique*, 1930. ≈ Opposite: the facade of the Blackstone. Its style and ornamentation would be imitated by virtually every hotel built in Chicago between 1908 and 1914. Inset: two telegrams signed by the Blackstone's management; one congratulating President Eisenhower, the other welcoming President Truman. Below: a tea party in the Blackstone, around 1950. Right page: Eisenhower arriving at the Blackstone in July 1952. It was during his stay here that he learned that the Republican Party had nominated him has their candidate for the presidency. Inset: Mamie Eisenhower, celebrating her husband's nomination in their suite.

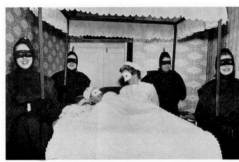

The two great Chicago hotels of the 1870s were the Palmer House and the Grand Pacific. The latter, founded by a certain Mr. Drake, though quite a success, attracted a rather run-of the-mill clientele. Forty years later Drake's sons, John and Tracy, opened the Blackstone which was to become a favorite with members of Chicago's high society. Even the most modern — and gigantic — hotels built in Chicago during the 20's could not rival the Blackstone. Small, compared to the newer hotels, the Blackstone provided unequalled privacy and comfort to its guest. A particular favorite with politicians, it was flatteringly referred to as "the hotel of presidents." Though the Blackstone, like the other great hotels of the city, welcomed the crowds that attended conventions and business meetings, it remained a bastion of tradition and elegance. It is said that the hotel manager opened his newspaper one morning to discover a picture of a hotel bellhop standing with his hands in his pockets. Infuriated by such slovenliness, he ordered that the trouser pockets of all male members of the staff be sewn closed by the next day.

≈ Above: costume party, 1950 Opposite : the Duke and Duchess of Windsor and the managing director of the Blackstone, around 1960. Below: menu from the Café Bonaparte. Right page: Lena Horne performing in the Mayfair Room, the hotel's nightclub until the Café Bonaparte opened in 1956. Following pages: the Drake (on the right), 1920.

FAR
WES

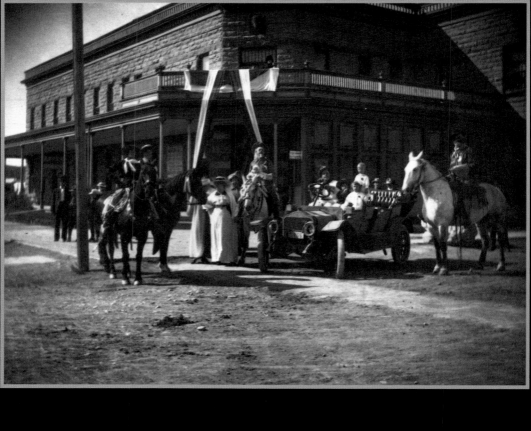

When John Colter, a former member of the Clark expedition (1804-1806), came back from a solo exploration of the Rockies, some people thought he had lost his mind. He spoke of a fabulous country with gigantic mountains and hot spring geysers that shot up into the sky. He had in fact been travelling in what was to become, in 1872, Yellowstone National Park. Such natural wonders have made Wyoming one of the most visited States in the country and incited the construction of two of the most astonishing hotels in the West: the Old Faithful and the Canyon. Urban centers in this same state, however, boasted few hotels of interest, although some of them, like the Plains in Cheyenne, used the title "grand hotel" – no doubt because it was the *only* hotel around! In Cody,

the Irma Hotel had nothing particular to recommend it but was *the* place to stay... the Irma and the town of Cody were both founded by W.F. Cody, alias Buffalo Bill. ≈ Above: the Plains Hotel. Opposite: staircase of the Canyon Hotel. Inset: invitation to the Irma, 1902. Left page, top: Buffalo Bill, his wife and grand children in front of the Irma in 1915; Bottom: facade and lobby of the Old Faithful Inn. Preceding pages: Colorado during the winter of 1899.

Virginia City, founded in 1859 and built on gold and silver from the Comstock Lode, was once the richest city in Nevada. The 1870s marked its prime. During those years, at night, the streets rang with music from the saloons, where fortunes were made and lost on the turn of a card or a roll of the dice. In 1877, at the corner of B and C streets (the city's founding fathers didn't waste any time searching for interesting street names...) a grand hotel was built. Called the International, it was six stories high, had a mansard roof with an elegant zinc counter-rail, and was furnished exactly like the Palace Hotel in San Francisco. Each room had Persian carpets and wall hangings and each floor was serviced by an hydraulic elevator – the first to be built in Nevada. On the ground floor there was a saloon, a restaurant and a spectacular cigar shop whose sign, in the shape of a giant cigar, spewed sparks from the "lit" end. Alas, when the ore began to run out, the hotel management had to revise its prices to accommodate the diminishing income of its guests – the city and its grand hotel were doomed. The International was finally destroyed by fire in 1914. Virginia City, which had a population of 30,000 in 1870, is now a town of only 600 inhabitants. ≈ Bottom: unidentified hotel in Virginia City. Inset: a menu from the original International Hotel that was replaced by the 1877 International. Opposite: unidentified hotel in Virginia City.

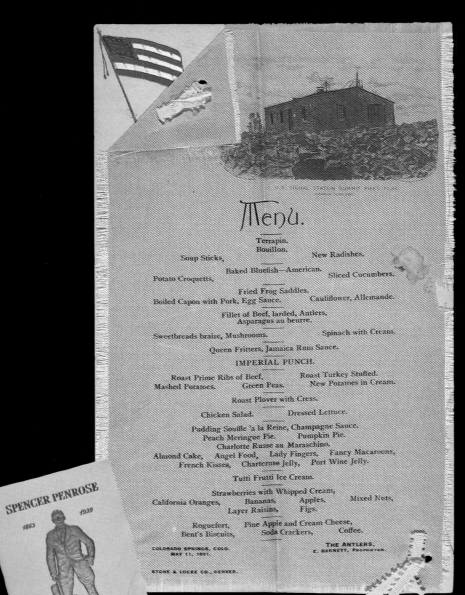

Menu.

Terrapin.
Bouillon.

Soup Sticks,   New Radishes.

Baked Bluefish—American.
Potato Croquetts,   Sliced Cucumbers.

Fried Frog Saddles.
Boiled Capon with Pork, Egg Sauce.   Cauliflower, Allemande.

Fillet of Beef, larded, Antlers,
Asparagus au beurre.

Sweetbreads braize, Mushrooms.   Spinach with Cream.

Queen Fritters, Jamaica Rum Sauce.

IMPERIAL PUNCH.

Roast Prime Ribs of Beef.   Roast Turkey Stuffed.
Mashed Potatoes.   Green Peas.   New Potatoes in Cream.

Roast Plover with Cress.

Chicken Salad.   Dressed Lettuce.

Pudding Souffle 'a la Reine, Champagne Sauce.
Peach Meringue Pie.   Pumpkin Pie.
Charlotte Russe au Maraschino.
Almond Cake,   Angel Food,   Lady Fingers,   Fancy Macaroons,
French Kisses,   Charteruse Jelly,   Port Wine Jelly.

Tutti Frutti Ice Cream.

Strawberries with Whipped Cream,
California Oranges,   Bananas,   Apples,   Mixed Nuts,
Layer Raisins,   Figs.

Roquefort,   Pine Apple and Cream Cheese,
Bent's Biscuits,   Soda Crackers,   Coffee.

COLORADO SPRINGS, COLO.
MAY 11, 1891.

THE ANTLERS,
E. BARNETT, Proprietor.

STONE & LOCKE CO., DENVER.

SPENCER PENROSE
1865   1939

The millionaire, Spencer Penrose, had stayed in many grand hotels but few satisfied him. The Antlers disappointed him so much that he decided to put it out of business by building his own grand hotel nearby. The new hotel, called the Broadmoor, opened in 1918 but prior to its official opening Penrose invited his most important friends and relations to come for an evening as his guests. To his dismay, John D. Rockefeller became violently ill when exposed to the odor of the still wet paint and had to make a rapid exit. The guest of honor spent the rest of the evening recuperating... at the Antlers.
≈ Above: facade and horseback riding club at the Broadmoor. Opposite: bird's-eye view of the hotel complex. Below: the original casino, opened in 1890 by the Count of Pourtales; this is now the site of the Broadmoor Golf Club. Left page: facade and menu belonging to the original Antlers (1890), and the cover of a pamphlet published in 1958 in memory of Spencer Penrose.

At the base of the Rocky Mountains, surrounded by fertile land, Boulder was a prosperous city at the turn of the century. Miners came here to buy provisions and the streets were crowded with horses and carriages transporting goods and people in a permanent cloud of dust. The town still reflected its modest beginnings as a frontier outpost and residents were clamoring for a more elegant atmosphere. In 1905, a member of the city council declared: "this city will never change unless we build a good hotel." In January of 1906, a campaign was begun to collect money for building just such an hotel. Even the local papers became involved: "Those who hold back", one editorialist wrote, "and look for enterprise by others are skulkers in the battalions of progress." The people of Boulder responded en masse and in April of 1906 the necessary funds had been raised. It was just the right time for work to begin, for a disastrous earthquake had recently struck San Francisco, destroying its finest establishments

– Colorado was soon to welcome visitors that its coastal cousin could no longer house. The new hotel, the Boulderado, was an instant success. When it opened in 1909, it put Boulder on the map.

≈ Above: Meeting held at the Boulderado, 1920. Left: the Boulderado as it looks today; the children of Hugh Mark, managing director from 1917 to 1934, in front of the hotel. Right: Christmas menu, and Fred Weber who was bellhop at the hotel in 1910.

Wherever gold or silver were discovered, town sprang up literally overnight. Frequently, the were really glorified mining camps and th hotels that opened in them, though profitab to operate, often provided little more than shelter: the first "hote to open in Aspen, in 1880, was simply a big tent in which "room were created by hanging blankets over ropes strung between pole Many of these mining towns would be deserted when the ore ra out, but others had brighter futures and developed into real cities. In the latter case, a sure sign of prosperity, and the beginnings of social stratification, was the building of a luxury hotel. In Durango, the elegant Strater opened in 1887, only six years after the city was founded. In Aspen, the town evolved at an equally rapid pace. In 1889 the town's fake wood facades and tumble-down houses gave way to sturdy stone structures; an Opera was built, and above all, a magnificent hotel was opened. The Jerome boasted 90 rooms, some of which, according to eye-witness accounts, were as sumptuous as any at the Ritz in Paris. ≈ Above and opposite: the facade and a room in the Strater. Inset and left page: the bar at the Jerome and the manager's daughters photographed in the lobby at Christmas time in 1916.

A ccording to an article in *Scientific American* published on May 22nd 1892, the architects commissioned to build the Brown Palace in Denver went through no less than two tons of paper in designing the hotel. Cleverly conceived, the Brown was built on a triangular plot of land in such a way that each room had a particularly pleasant view of the city. Indeed, to fully satisfy each guest, visitors were asked if they preferred rooms facing the rising or setting sun. This was but one of the many touches that distinguished the Brown Palace which remains, to this day, the epitome of the grand hotel. The main lobby is a splendid atrium, surrounded by six floors of metal-beamed galleries held up by onyx pillars that rise to an immense glass roof. ≈ Above: the former presidential suite where Theodore Roosevelt, William Howard Taft, Franklin D. Roosevelt and many

other heads of State stayed. Among the Kings and Queens that visited the Brown one could cite Mary of Romania, the Prince of Sweden and the King and Queen of Denmark. Inset, left, the Brown's facade and, right, the hotel under construction. Only fireproof material was used (ovenfired brick and metal beams domi-

nated). Opposite: a prize-winner at the State Fair, photographed at the hotel's reception desk. Left page, top, cocktail party honoring the U.S. Air Force in the 1940s; bottom, fireplace in the lobby, around 1930.

The Oxford Hotel, which opened in 1891, was designed by the architect F.E. Edbrooke. A year later, Edbrooke would build his masterpiece, the Brown Palace. Denver was then the third largest city in the West (the two others were San Francisco and Omaha). At the juncture of more than a hundred railway lines, Denver was a logical place for travellers to stop for a rest. To accommodate the most elegant, the Oxford was built very near Union Station. Its relatively plain facade gave no hint of the hotel's extravagant interior: the light filtering down from the glass roof flooded an area decorated with marble, murals, and silver chandeliers – a foreshadowing of the kind of luxury guests would encounter later in the Brown Palace. The Oxford would be renovated on several occasions; among the most successful was the 1930 renovation in *Art Deco style*. ≈ Above: the hotel facade. Opposite and below: the coffee shop at the Oxford with its stained glass windows; postcard and luggage label. Right page: the *Art Deco* bar at the Oxford built to resemble one of the lounges on the Queen Mary.

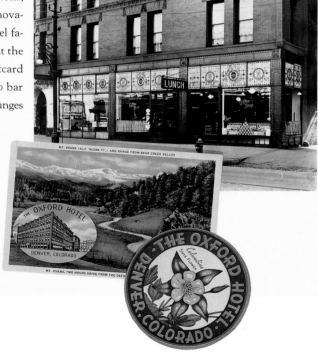

In Arizona and New Mexico, the survival of pre-Colombian cultures and the presence of some very strange natural wonders led to the creation of most unusual hotels. Buildings in the "Mission Style" or the "Toltec Style" typically open onto magnificent panoramas or cool, shaded patios. These hotels, which often made the most of a varied landscape and the natural resources in their vicinity, were to win the praises of Simone de Beauvoir, who generally despised American hotels. Of one such establishment, located in the hot plains of New Mexico, she wrote: "The La Fonda is the most beautiful hotel in America, perhaps the most beautiful I have ever seen in my life. The patio is surrounded by cool walkways paved with a mosaic of tiles and Spanish-style furnishings; here, an Indian stands in the lobby who has been selling fake turquoise and pieces of petrified wood to tourists for years." From, *L'Amérique au jour le jour.* ≈ Above: the El Tovar hotel in the Grand Canyon National Park, Arizona. Inset, below and following pages: the swimming pool, the lobby and main entrance to the Arizona Biltmore in Phoenix, Arizona. Right page, top: facade of the Bishop's Lodge in 1930. This hotel

was built several miles north of Santa Fe in 1917 on land that once belonged to the Catholic church; bottom, brochure published in the 1930s in which the La Fonda appears. The La Fonda, which opened in the 1920s, was owned by the Santa Fe Railway; note the architect's use of traditional motifs, reproduced here in concrete rather than adobe.

LA FONDA

Santa Fe, New Mexico

The Harvey Company

LA FONDA

Santa Fe, New Mexico

The Harvey Company

The Skirvin Hotel, Ok-
lahoma City, in 1915
and one of its guests,
the poet Carl Sand-
burg, in 1938. Right page, top:
the governor of Oklahoma in the

Lee-Huckins Hotel, Oklahoma
City, on the 12th of June 1910, the
day after Oklahoma City was
declared the capital of the State;
bottom, staff of the Park Hotel,
Sulphur Springs.

"I was told that the Menger was the most respectable and comfortable hotel in town. When I arrived it was full. Nonetheless, since every room had two beds, it was suggested that I share a room with another gentleman. I was assured that such an arrangement would not inconvenience either of us and that this was common practice in San Antonio. Since I only planned to stay one night (and having gotten used to a wide variety of company on the Pullman), I resigned myself to this solution... In the courtyard, even before the hot sun graced us with its rays, the banana trees reminded me that this was a semi-tropical region and there was no escaping the heat." A. Maufroid, *Du Mexique au Canada*, 1907. ≈ Other Texas hotels: <u>above</u>, lobby of the Texas State Hotel in Houston and <u>inset,</u>facade of the St. Anthony International (simply called the St. Anthony when it opened in 1909); <u>opposite,</u> lobby of the Lancaster in Houston, around 1930; <u>right page,</u> lounge in the Plaza Hotel, San Antonio, around 1920.

TO THE
PACIFIC

San Francisco's Palace Hotel was built in 1875. It dominated the City and was internationally renowned, but certain customers, like Rudyard Kipling, were irritated by the manners in the American West: "When the hotel clerk – the man who awards your room to you and who is supposed to give you information – when that resplendent individual stoops to attend to your wants, he does so whistling, or humming or picking his teeth, or pauses to coverse

with someone he knows. These performances, I gather, are to impress upon you that he is a free man and your equal. In a vast marble-paved hall under the glare of an electric light sat forty or fifty men, and for their use and amusement were provided spittoons of infinite capacity and generous gape. Most of the men wore frock coats and top hats – the things that we in India put on at a wedding breakfast if we possessed them but they all spat..." *From Sea to Sea*, 1899 ≃ <u>Above</u>: the Palace Hotel (left) and the city, in 1880;

and the hotel in flames on the day of the April, 1906 earthquake. <u>Opposite, left</u>: the Market Street facade around 1900. <u>Right page</u>: the entry courtyard, around 1890; this splendid atrium, was one of San Francisco's liveliest spots. <u>Following pages</u>: the first building, destroyed by the fire, was reconstructed in 1909 and rechristened the Sheraton Palace Hotel in 1954: here, the main dining room which occupies the site of the former entry courtyard. <u>Preceding pages</u>: the St.Francis (foreground) and naval vessels with shining lights, December 7, 1941.

In 1926, the owner of the Fairmont was looking for a way to increase his income. He decided to built a luxurious penthouse suite on the hotel roof and hired Arthur Upham Hope as a consultant. Hope was then a professor at Berkeley and a specialist in Oriental Art. The two men created an eight-room suite entirely decorated in the most sumptuous Middle Eastern style: walls covered with mosaics, arched doorways, fireplaces inlaid with lapis lazuli and ceilings decorated with stars. This apartment was to become the home of Mrs. Maude Flood, daughter-in-law of James Flood (who had made a fortune in the gold mines of the famous Comstock Lode). Mrs Flood occupied the penthouse for thirty years but, since 1981, it has been free for anyone who wishes to rent it for one night or more. The hotel management, however, decline to reveal the identity of the privileged few who have stayed there; after all, one night costs a whopping five thousand dollars... without tax. ≈ Above and opposite: a lounge and game room in the penthouse suite; the suite has a private terrace overlooking the city. Left page: the Fairmont lobby.

"An hour later, we found about a dozen of our compatriots in the Tea Room of the St. Francis. It had been ages since we had seen a room of this size, full of elegant people, laughing and free from the worries that had weighed so heavily on even the most frivolous of us for so many years. There, for the first time, I really felt that the war was over." Joseph Kessel, *Dames de Californie.* ≈ Above: washing coins. This became customary at the St. Francis starting in 1938. Every shopkeeper and taxi driver in town knew that the shiny coins they were handed had, at one time, gone through the "laundry" at the famous hotel. Below: a guest arriving at the St. Francis for a fashion show. Opposite: dinner-dance in the great dining room decorated with its famous murals (hence its name, "The Mural Room"), in the 1940s.

CERES NEPTVN

13441
WEAVER

On September 19th, 1923, about a hundred famous hotel owners, including John Bowman who was President of the Biltmore chain, left New York's Grand Central Station in private railway cars. The 1st of October, they arrived in Los Angeles just in time for the inaugural ball in that city's new grand hotel: the Biltmore. More than three thousand people attended the affair; beautiful ladies were exquisitely dressed and escorted by the wealthiest and most powerful businessmen in the country. Miss Peggy Hamilton, a fashion-setter whose taste was highly esteemed, was a star attraction. That evening she wore a hand-painted dress of Florentine satin with a front panel painted to resemble a portion of the Crystal Ballroom ceiling at the Biltmore. The broad pockets that stuck out on either side of the dress not only rounded her hips but were decorated with painted replicas of the balconies in the ballroom. To complete this *ensemble*, Miss Hamilton wore jeweled copies of the ballroom's chandeliers in her blond hair. Little wonder that, in the years to follow, the hotel management would invite Miss Hamilton – nicknamed "The Biltmore Girl" – to exhibit her "architectural" costume on numerous occasions. ≈ Above, left, the Biltmore facade; right, Miss Vada Heilman. Before the Biltmore was opened to the public, she was assigned the awesome task of making sure that all 4400 hotel keys did indeed fit their corresponding locks. Below: Miss Peggy Hamilton in her famous dress; to her left is Giovanni Smeraldi who designed the ceiling in the Crystal Ballroom and, to her right, Florence Gilbert who painted Miss Hamilton's dress. Left page: entrance to the Biltmore on Olive Street, around 1940.

The Biltmore was designed by Schultze & Weaver, the same architects who built the Waldorf-Astoria. When it opened, with its 13 stories and 1100 rooms, it was the largest hotel west of Chicago. Recent renovations, costing a total of 40 million dollars, have restored the hotel to its former glory while preserving the original decor. ≈ <u>Above</u>: the men's room, 1923. <u>Opposite</u>: front cover of a menu on which the staircase in the "Rendezvous Court" is pictured, and <u>below</u>, landing on this same staircase. <u>Right page</u>: the "Gallery Bar".

If the Beverly Hills has been one of the most famous hotels in the world since 1912, it is neither because it is architecturally interesting or particularly well equipped. Its renown is due to the number of famous people and movie stars who have lived there at one time or another. The hotel management still forbids picture-taking inside the hotel and furnishes virtually no information about its occupants. ≈ Opposite: the Beverly Hills' pink facade, pictured behind a double rampart of shrubbery and masonry. Above: a maid at the Hollywood Roosevelt. Called simply the Roosevelt when it opened in 1927, it was once the center of social activity in Hollywood.

Hotels of Bel Air, Hollywood or Beverly Hills project images of themselves which tend to obscure their shortcomings. Even a casual stroller in the Bel-Air gardens will notice the hideous cement walkways and the plastic that covers the patios. But no one seems to care. Guests, intoxicated by the odor of the magnolia blossoms, are perfectly content to lounge in the shade of the palm trees without giving a second thought to such "minor" imperfections. A similar attitude is encountered at the venerable, but slightly worn, Chateau Marmont. Its dust is simply considered one of its "charms". Like Carole Lombard, Jane Harlow, Marilyn Monroe or James Dean before them, today's visitors are enchanted by this mysterious building perched on a hill overlooking Sunset Boulevard. ≈ Above: a lounge in the Bel-Air Hotel. Inset and below: gardens and a lounge at the Beverly Hills Hotel. Right page: the veranda of the Chateau Marmont (opened in 1927).

"But does it really matter, darling," says the middle-aged, muu-muu clad lady from Cleveland with the huge red hibiscus flowers behind her right ear, "that there's no longer running pineapple juice in the drinking fountains at the Royal Hawaiian Hotel? Or that most of the sand at Waikiki Beach is trucked over from someplace else?" *Hawaii* Insight Guides, 1987. ≃ Like Miami, Hawaii has become one of those artificial paradises where people search to no avail for the exotic atmosphere described in the dazzling accounts of Mark Twain or Robert Louis Stevenson. They will find few parallels in the concrete walls now lining the Waikiki beachfront. Nevertheless, traces of charm manage to survive : on the Hotel Moana's terrace guests can relish the cool shade of a Banyan fig tree; at the Halekulani they discover a pearly sea shell on their pillows every evening. And, like a jewel in a setting of skyscrapers, the Royal Hawaiian's pink cupola is still one of the last bastions of the exotic fantasy. ≃ Above: Hula dancers in the Royal Hawaiian's palm court, and the hotel's facade. Opposite. Royal Hawaiian guests; an American sailor on leave, 1942, and Shirley Temple, 1935. Inset: "Baby Moana", who went on to become a star of the silent screen, was born in the Moana Hotel in 1903; she was named after this elegant establishment where her parents worked. Left page: American tourists in Hawaii, 1920s.

"To ride the backs of the waves, rise out of the foam to stand full length in the air above and with heels winged with the swiftness of horses to fly shoreward, was what made sport for them and brought them out from Honolulu to Waikiki." Jack London, *The Kanaka Surf*, 1916. ≃ <u>Above</u>: the Moana Hotel's ocean-front facade around 1930. <u>Below</u>: surfing instructors on Waikiki Beach, 1946; surfing was one of the favorite activities of the hotels' guests. <u>Right page</u>: shortly after the attack on Pearl Harbor, the Royal Hawaiian was requisitioned by the U.S. Marines, who used it as a rest and relaxation center: here, soldiers who have momentarily gotten rid of their helmets and gas masks. <u>Following pages</u>: the Royal Hawaiian's inauguration day, February 1, 1927.

Edgeworth
Photo

When the old railway hand Morley Roberts went back to Banff during the summer of 1925, he hardly recognized the place he had left 42 years before. Station Number 29 of the Canadian Pacific Railroad, which he remembered so vividly, was now called Banff. The dusty camp set up at the foot of Cascade Mountain had become one of the most famous holiday resorts in North America.

Even more surprises were in store for Morley. Not far from the village, overlooking the Bow River Valley, lost in the immense wilderness of the Rocky Mountains, he discovered a castle. The citadel was built of dark limestone, flanked by massive towers, and adorned with turrets, arches, and gables. The pile of masonry seemed so out of place, so incongruous, that the old railway worker was indignant. Forty years earlier, no one in his right mind would have dreamed of building such an unlikely structure in such an improbable place.

This dream-like fortress is the Banff Springs Hotel, and since Morley's visit many other travellers have been as astounded as the railway worker was the first time he laid eyes on its extravagant architecture. Banff Springs Hotel, however, is far from being just a castle in the air; on the contrary, it is part of a well-calculated strategy thought up by the Canadian Pacific Railway Company. For decades, this company mustered its skills and energy to face the Canadian challenge. By 1886, a traveller could go from Montreal to Vancouver non-

CANADA
THE CITADELS
—of the—
TRANSCANADIAN
—by—
CATHERINE DONZEL
Translation by Glenn Naumovitz

stop: the Canadian Pacific had turned the dream of national unity into a concrete reality by linking the two coasts of this vast country. And, by 1888, the Canadian Pacific Railway was helping to forge an authentic Canadian cultural identity by exporting the image of the castle-hotels that sprang up all along the line until the 1930s. The Banff Springs, Chateau Lake Louise, Chateau Frontenac, the Royal York and the Empress of Victoria were explicitly designed as monuments erected to the glory of a young nation on the move. Their distinctive château style would even influence Canada's official architecture, and the history of these great hotels is inseparable from the dynamics that led the country into modernity.

LINKING EAST AND WEST
Canada's constitution had been ratified by the British Parliament in 1867 but at that time, the confederation's existence was still only theoretical. The majority of the population lived in the eastern provinces of Quebec, Ontario, New Brunswick and Nova Scotia. Ottawa had little control over the rest of Canadian territory. Manitoba was an immense, still largely unexplored region. Its Indian and mixed race populations became hostile to the Canadian government, which annexed the area in 1869 without consulting them. In addition, sparsely populated British Columbia, isolated on the Pacific coast by the Rocky Mountains, was attracting America's attention. Clearly, it was essential to create a single nation out of this geographical and political puzzle. No less important was keeping British Columbia from giving

1. A poster commemorating sixty years of Canadian Pacific service, 1945.
2. CPR brochure, 1893.
3. Banff village, 1910.
Left page: the Château Frontenac, 1899.

in to the advances of its strong southern neighbor.

National unity, some argued, could only be achieved by physically linking the provinces through the construction of a Canadian transcontinental railway. The idea

for such a railway had been in the air for years and Canadians had been observing with interest American attempts to link their two coastlines. Defenders of the Canadian project pointed with satisfaction to the completion of the American transcontinental railway on May 10, 1869. On that historic date, the Central Pacific Railway, working eastward and the Union Pacific, working westward, met at Promontory Point in Utah, closing the final 1,800 mile gap that separated Omaha, Nebraska from San Francisco. Despite the impact of this engineering feat, opponents warned that the expense of financing such a project in Canada would "lead the country to ruin." Prime Minister John Alexander MacDonald, however, believed that the future of Canada depended upon the creation of a transcanadian railway and, in 1870, he made one of the rashest

promises in history: he assured British Columbia that 4,700 kilometers (2,920 miles) of railway would be built in order to link the province to the rest of the continent. This commitment finally convinced the wavering Pacific coast settlers to opt for joining the Confederation in 1871.

The years went by. Even though fulfilling the promise of the much talked-about line was more pressing than ever, not a single stretch of track had been laid. Western Canada's isolation at a

time when the East was undergoing an economic boom fostered resentment and heated tempers. British Columbia threatened to secede. Delighted by the turn of events, the Americans had begun eying the Canadian Northwest and debating the feasability of its eventual annexation. The atmosphere in Parliament grew stormier day by day as MacDonald's promise seemed impossible to keep. Investors were worried about the

project's financial prospects. They feared that traffic on a railroad crossing vast, uninhabited expanses covered with ice seven months out of the year would be non-existent. Finally, the Indian and mixed race populations in Manitoba were arming themselves to prevent construction of a line that would disperse

buffalo herds and seemed to be yet another manifestation of colonial domination.

Nonetheless, in 1872 two rival companies were formed, each hoping to obtain a government contract for the construction of the railway. When the head of one company, Sir Hugh Alan, was accused and convicted of bribing government officials in 1873, suspicion surrounded everyone implicated in the project. MacDonald was forced to resign as prime minister, though there was no proof of any wrong doing on his part, and a new government was formed. Work on the railway came to a premature halt.

Political opponents had declared in 1874 that "John A. has fallen, never to rise again", but five years later MacDonald returned to office and in 1878 he made the completion of the railroad one of his new government's top priorities. On February 15, 1881, he signed a $25,000,000 contract with the

1. "Rocky Mountains Landscape", a watercolor by Lucius O'Brien, 1888. 2. William Cornelius Van Horne. 3. Driving in the last spike on the Canadian-Pacific line, November 7, 1885. 4. Railway workers, around 1885. 5. The CPR hired many painters and photographers to illustrate its advertising campaigns; here, the specially equipped convoy for the Notman brothers; one of the wagons was equipped with a dark room.

newly formed Canadian Pacific Railway (CPR), including a 25 million – acre concession of land along the route for the company to sell or develop. The CPR committed itself to finishing construction in ten years time. This seemingly impossible task might never been accomplished save for the drive and perseverance of one man – Cornelius Van Horne. Then only 38 years old, Van Horne was an American of Dutch descent. This former office boy was to master-mind the project and carry it to completion after George Stephen, president of the CPR, appointed him General Director of the company in 1881. Van Horne would rise rapidly in the ranks of the company, becoming president by 1888.

When he began his career with the CPR, Van Horne was no newcomer to the world of railroads. He had already acquired a solid background in several American railroad companies, including the Chicago-Milwaukee and St. Paul line. He had his own way of getting things done. He attacked problems head-on and seemed to be everywhere at the same time: he was seen encouraging the railroad workers (sometimes spending whole nights playing poker with them), appeasing the

project's critics, and reassuring its investors. Van Horne did his job so well, in fact, that the last spike of the Canadian Pacific was driven in on November 7th, 1885, nearly five years ahead of the deadline negotiated by the company and the federal government. At the inauguration ceremony, Van Horne's speech was typically short and to the point: "All that I can say is that the work has been well done in every way".

OUTDOING PULLMAN

Although all of the track had been laid, Van
Horne knew that the work had just begun; much
remained to be done before the railroad would be
operational. The ballast had only been partially laid,
stations had to be built and, in the West, the new
tracks were already threatened by avalanches. Once
again, he would have to work miracles, especially
since George Stephen had promised the company's
shareholders that the Canadian Pacific would be in
service by the Spring of 1886.

The railroad's construction costs were staggering,
and these "finishing touches"
promised to be very expensive, too: around $6.2 million
for 1886 alone (in compari-
son, a railroad worker earned
a $1.50 a day at the time).
Making the line profitable
was essential. Hopes for the
coast's economic develop-
ment were pinned on setting
up reliable service which
would spur a "stampede to the Canadian West". The
CPR agencies had already launched a promotional
campaign in both Europe and North America,
encouraging immigration. But Van Horne also hoped
to draw another breed of customers: lovers of luxury
trains, people who wouldn't fret about expense and
would not hesitate to come back. In other words, he
was aiming for the well-to-do tourist.

The groundwork for future tourism was laid even
while the line was under construction. During the
winter of 1885-6, Van Horne sent observation teams
into British Columbia's Selkirk Mountains. The
reports he received were hardly encouraging: one
team counted nine avalanches on just one section of
track, and another observed that, in some places, the
rails had disappeared under 39 feet of snow. Drawing
on his experience acquired south of the border, Van
Horne resorted to a solution previously used by the
American Central Pacific Railway. He had sturdy
shelters built to cover the tracks wherever they were

threatened by landslides, rockslides, and snow. Work
began immediately and by the end of 1886, thirty of
these structures, located along 5 miles of track,
guaranteed the safe passage of trains through the
Selkirk Mountains. The drawback was that 5 miles of
spectacular mountain scenery would be lost to view,
including the breathtaking panorama of the Illecillewaet Valley, which alone was worth the trip. Van
Horne had no trouble finding a solution: a second
set of rails was constructed wherever the first one was
covered. The view was saved, at least for those
travelling during the summer months.

Nothing was impossi-
ble for such a determined
and ingenious man. Van
Horne looked after essen-
tials and minor details
alike. Even in the hostile
environment of the Rock-
ies, he finished the rail
improvements before the
deadline set by Stephen.
The first passenger train
bound for the West Coast, the "Pacific Express", left
Montreal at 8 p.m. on June 28, 1886. Six days later,
at noon on July 4, it pulled into Port Moody, around
12 miles from Vancouver. A sleeping and dining car
accompanied the Pacific Express on its maiden voyage.

Both the cars and the service were thoughtfully
designed. The Canadian Pacific was the longest and

1. The CPR took
part in a number
of fairs and
international
exhibitions during
the 1880s; here, a
painting by John
Fraser, "The
Rogers Pass",
probably
commissioned by
George Stephen for
the 1886 London
Colonial
Exhibition.
2. Interior of a
first-class car.

194

probably most comfortable railroad in the world at the time.

The second and "Colonist" classes, the cheapest and best-suited to the immigrant's budget, offered passengers a bare-bones but reasonably comfortable

journey, according to contemporary accounts. First class, however, spared no luxury in its quest for first place among international rail standards. Van Horne, who never shrank from a challenge, ordered the firm in charge of constructing the CPR's custom-built cars to make the sleeping berths longer and wider than Pullman's, then the undisputed champion of rail comfort.

The dining cars were just as carefully designed. Gleaming copper wall fittings, inlaid wood paneling, embossed leather seats, and the finest linen and silverware complemented the impeccable service. On top of these refinements, taking the Canadian Pacific amounted to a chef's tour of the continent. Menus

varied depending on the region being crossed, from St. Lawrence trout to Fraser River salmon. All of these delicacies were washed down with excellent imported wines, assuring an idyllic voyage.

Unfortunately, things went downhill as soon as the trains hit the Rockies. There hadn't been enough time to drill mountain tunnels, which turned the trip into a perilous roller coaster ride. The locomotives

had to climb slopes that were twice as steep as the acceptable standard. Eating in the dining cars during an ascent or descent became practically impossible : silverware rattled alarmingly, and plates and glasses went flying. Worse still, these cars were so heavy that eventually it was decided to leave them at the bottom of the slopes. A series of "dining-stations" was built, and the CPR hotel system was born.

DINING-STATIONS AND SWISS CHALETS

Initially, three dining-stations were built in the Rockies near the run's most arduous stretches. Passengers momentarily deprived of a dining car could have their meals in comfort. But beyond mere gastronomic considerations, their lofty locations offered travellers the sweeping spectacle of the Rocky Mountains. Mount Stephen House in

Kicking Horse Valley was completed in October, 1886. Glacier House, at the foot of the Illecillewaet Glacier, and Fraser Canyon House in North Bend opened in January, 1887. A British architect named Thomas Sorby designed all three buildings along the same lines: a central, three-story bay flanked by a pair of asymmetrical wings. Mount Stephen House, originally containing six or seven rooms, turned the composition around, and there were two dining rooms instead of one. These dining-stations were charming, though a bit rudimentary. The extensive

1. Interior of a dining car. 2. Mount Stephen House, Field, British Columbia, around 1886. 3. Poster informing passengers that a special service had been set up between Toronto and Chicago for the 1893 World's Fair.

use of wood, lively colors, and intricate carvings were combined to stress the windows and eaves, evoking Swiss chalet architecture. The reference was deliberate. Van Horne, who worked closely with Sorby, seized the opportunity to make one of his

long-held dreams come true: turning the Rockies into the New World equivalent of the Swiss Alps. In Europe, the Alps were becoming an increasingly popular tourist destination. The first Alpine Club, founded in London, chose Switzerland to train its members in 1860. The English vacation industry pioneer, Thomas Cook, organized his first tour there in 1863; it became his most popular offering. Van Horne saw that the time was ripe. He launched a promotional campaign organized around the theme of "the Canadian Alps", astutely predicting that the Rockies would soon tempt Europeans.

A number of organizational problems had to be worked out when the dining-stations opened. Service depended on the train schedule. The slightest variation resulted in total confusion, and soon the CPR began receiving complaints. Management was

informed that the restaurant service at Glacier House left much to be desired. If a westbound and eastbound train were unable to respect the timetable for some reason and pulled in at the same time, the otherwise enjoyable stopover turned into a real nightmare. The passengers were packed into crowded dining rooms like cattle, where they waited in vain to be served. All it took was the sound of grinding wheels to send them scrambling for the door, pushing and shoving one another out of fear of being left behind. Directives were sent to the personnel telling them to reassure travellers that, no matter what happened, they would not be left stranded on the platform in the middle of the mountains with empty stomachs.

These facilities quickly outgrew the role of mountain refuge or dining-station and became elegant resort hotels. The additions built during the years following their initial construction clearly attest to their growing popularity. People came alone or in groups for a few days of recreation and fresh air. After an excursion or croquet game in the hotel garden, the typical day would end in quiet conversation on the veranda. No one seemed to mind the roaring thunder of the occasional passing train. The heyday of these establishments was around the turn of the century; their popularity began to decline a little after 1910. Newly-built tunnels rerouted the trains, leaving the hotels off the beaten track. They eventually fell into disuse. Glacier House, the most famous of the three, was torn down in 1930. But in the meantime, the CPR added new hotels to its chain, better geared to Van Horne's objectives.

1. Fraser Canyon House in North Bend, 1887. 2. A CPR advertising poster, 1895. 3. Cricket players on the Glacier House lawn, 1920.

SELLING THE SCENERY

The needs of travellers to and from the new towns gradually

sprouting up along the railway line had to be taken into account as well. Villages exploded into big cities almost overnight; Vancouver is a case in point. In 1887 it replaced Port Moody as the Canadian Pacific's Western terminus. And that's where Van Horne built his first urban hotel, named after the city itself (this was not the present-day Vancouver Hotel,

built between 1928 and 1939). Once again Thomas Sorby was in charge of drawing up the plans, but he was not happy with the results: in his own words, it

had been built "without architecture". Indeed, the finished hotel spurred controversy. Some critics compared it to "an exceedingly ugly workhouse"; others saw it as "a solid, rather plain structure, a sort of glorified farmhouse, to which a number of extra stories had been added".

The hotel was clearly needed, but as usual Van Horne was more concerned about the Rockies. His interest in the Canadian West, however, does not mean that he overlooked the touristic potential of other regions. On the contrary, he had intended to establish a coast-to-coast hotel chain from the outset. Of course he preferred the Rockies, which he somewhat tenderly referred to as "our mountains". But this superb yet unhospitable region did not appear to have much commercial potential, meaning that it would probably not turn a profit for the company, either. Since he couldn't sell ice and rocks,

he embarked on selling the scenery. The timing couldn't have been better. Europeans had fallen in love with the mountains. Philosophers, hygienists, and writers extolled the virtues of snow-capped peaks. According to the great nineteenth-century British esthete John Ruskin, "Mountains are the beginning and the end of natural landscape". Meanwhile the United States was beginning to discover the grandeur of its lands: Yellowstone became its first national park in 1872.

The time was ripe for tapping the tourist market. However, the most demanding — and richest — potential clients still had to be won over. The wealthy English traveller was used to roaming the Empire without ever leaving the lap of luxury. He was very attached to the thousand and one comforts that cushioned his daily life. Even in the middle of

1. Management and employees posing in front of the entrance of the first Vancouver Hotel, May 1888. 2. The same hotel's facade with the veranda on the right; this porch was so popular with Vancouver residents that hotel guests had a hard time finding rocking chairs for themselves! Management solved the problem by allowing only hotel guests to use the chairs and spittoons. 3. In the Rockies, 1920s.

the Rockies he had to be welcomed with the same quality of service that he would have enjoyed in Singapore or Bombay. He would undoubtedly like to

show his mettle by hunting bears or climbing a perilous glacier, as long as an excellent cup of tea, his usual newspapers, and a luxurious, familiar setting were waiting for him when he returned in the

of hot springs with renowned medicinal properties further opened up hopeful prospects. Spas were in vogue and every traveller was a potential customer. Finally, the Banff train station was nearby, which paved the way for the site's rapid development.

Van Horne wasn't the only one responsible for turning the Banff Springs Hotel into a success. The New York architect Bruce Price played a role that was at least as important by laying down the tenets of a new architectural style. The CPR commissioned

evening. For all these reasons, Van Horne felt the need to invent a kind of hotel that had never been seen before: one that combined monumental architecture and a magnificent natural setting.

Price for the first time in 1886. He was hired to design Windsor Station in Montreal. The company must have been impressed by the lounge cars he had designed for the Pennsylvania and Boston & Albany line. In any case, Van Horne was fascinated by

THE CANADIAN "CHATEAU"

Van Horne decided to build the Banff Springs Hotel in the newly-created Rocky Mountains Park (later renamed Banff National Park), at the spot where the Spray and Bow Rivers meet. He finally found a project big enough to fulfill both his own ambition and the needs of his clientele. It took a man of his boldness and imagination to foresee that this remote place was destined to become one of the most famous, elegant meeting places of the international elite. He did have a few hints, though. The setting's dramatic beauty was in perfect harmony with the "Wagnerian" taste of the day. The discovery

1. The CPR set up a camp system for hikers and mountain climbers alongside its hotel network. Hikers could have their meals and spend the night in these shelters, which were provided with rudimentary conveniences. Initiated in the Rockies, this idea later caught on in the hunting and fishing regions of Ontario. Here, a room at the Nipigon River camp, Ontario, 1923. 2. A view of the Bow River Valley from the Banff Springs Hotel. 3. The "new" Banff train station, 1888.

architecture and must have been familiar with Price's work, for he already had an established reputation.

Price submitted the plans for the Banff Springs Hotel in the summer of 1886. The foundations were dug that winter and construction began during the spring of 1887. Hundreds of workers, most of them

Chinese, were brought in to do the work.

The name of the construction site foreman has been lost to history, but one thing is certain: he would never forget Van Horne's arrival in the summer of 1887. Although the buildings were going up quickly, for some unknown reason the orientation of the floor plan had been turned around. The panoramic rotunda had a view of an unattractive slope of Sulphur Mountain. The kitchens, on the other hand, offered a spectacular view of Bow Valley. That day the normally calm, easy-going Van Horne exploded. But even while his thunderous voice was still echoing throughout the site, he had already drawn up plans for a second rotunda to be built behind the kitchens. Future guests were doubtless unaware of this near disaster. Other occasions also give an idea of Van Horne's architectural skill and legendary speed at making decisions. Shortly after the rotunda episode, he was asked for plans for the new Banff train station. Supposedly, he grabbed a piece of paper, dashed a few bold lines on it, and wrote on the back: "Take good tree trunks. Cut them up, bark

them and build your station."

In June 1888, the modern, 250-room Banff Springs Hotel was ready to welcome its first guests. The CPR's advertising brochures eagerly portrayed their new hotel as "the most beautiful on the whole North American continent".

The building consisted of two five-story wings. The top floor was incorporated into a mansard roof. The Van Horne Pavilion, facing the valley, stood detached from the rest of the building. Like the ones previously constructed in the Rockies, the facade blended light yellows with the warm brown hues of cedar. In more ways than one, the overall composition and design brought to mind Swiss chalet architecture. But its enormous size, corner turrets, projecting corbels, and bay windows lent the building the dignified bearing of a baronial manor.

The stylistic influences on Price's work have been the object of debate. Some feel that one of this sources was German palace architecture. Others detect a cross between a Swiss chalet and a Tudor Hall. Still others claim that Price was sending an overtly political message: in stylistically borrowing from the Loire Valley châteaux, they argue, the Banff Springs Hotel could be viewed as "a gesture of recognition to the French Canadian population and the French explorers who had blazed the trail for the Canadian Pacific." Van Horne certainly would never have committed the diplomatic blunder of labelling his hotel this way. It was far from Quebec and attracted a largely English clientele. But the allusion to the Loire Valley châteaux is not unfounded. Price had travelled widely in Europe and knew France well. The strength and

1. An overall view of the Banff Springs Hotel in 1888. 2. and 3. In 1904, the Canadian government began publishing its first tourist brochures, joining forces with the CPR in an effort to promote the Rockies; these pamphlets boasted about the mountains' natural beauty as well as the Canadian-Pacific's hotels.

grace expressed by these masterpieces no doubt influenced Banff Springs as well as many of Price's later works.

Aside from a few obvious influences like these, however, it is difficult to determine Price's sources of inspiration. To highlight the beauty of the setting and meet Van Horne's requirements, he relied on the picturesque, calling upon devices and allusions that he knew would stir the visitors' emotions and elicit their admiration. The Banff Springs Hotel of 1888 was a very early example of the "chateau style", a theatrical style meant to charm and impress.

The chateau style soon became much more than a CPR trademark; it would embody the Canadian national identity for several decades to come. Since it could bestow the evocative power of a historic landmark on any building, it was well-suited to this fledgling nation in search of cultural moorings and a common past.

Guests were unanimously enthusiastic at the inauguration of the Banff Springs Hotel. The new creation was lauded as "comfortable and daring", "a most sumptuous affair, as palatial as a Monterey or Saratoga hotel", "a wonder of art and invention in the wilderness". Less than twenty years later, the hotel register listed guests hailing from all four corners of the globe: South Africa, France, Austria, England, Japan, Borneo, Hong Kong, and of course the United States.

AROUND THE WORLD WITH CPR

Starting in 1886, the CPR flooded Europe and the United States with continually updated, adapted, and revised advertising material. Large, colorful posters depicting landscapes in Alberta or British Columbia

showed up on the walls of international capitals, stirring up dreams or fostering travel plans. Naive by today's standards, the slogans that went with the images seemed irresistibly innovative at the time and aroused the interest of even the most jaded travellers: "What the Duke said to the Prince: All sensible people travel on the CPR", "Parisian Politeness on the CPR" and others enticed the upper crust to travel on a line where they would meet only "the best people".

These efforts were rewarded in the 1890s. Despite the economic recession which darkened the decade, tourists from all over the world continued flocking to Canada. The growing number of sleeping and dining cars testifies to this increasing traffic. The Transcontinental began operating with 47 of these cars: in 1890 there were 61. And when the effects of the economic crisis first began to hit, 99 sleeping and dining cars were in service. It was time for the company to catch its breath.

The CPR soon offered its clients a new, attractive deal: a round-the-world tour by rail and sea. The Transcanadian already handled the journey from the Atlantic to Vancouver. Now the idea was to start up a regular Pacific maritime service from Vancouver to the Orient.

In 1891 three superb, 6,000-ton capacity ships set sail. Thanks to agreements with other rail and steamship companies, the CPR soon offered a regular

1. The Banff Springs Hotel of 1888 could hardly be called "chateau style" when compared to the 1928 construction which was much closer to what Van Horne had dreamed of. Here, Mount Stephen Hall, (lounge designed in the 1920s), presents all the caracteristics of an authentic baronial manor. 2. A poster for CPR Pacific cruises.

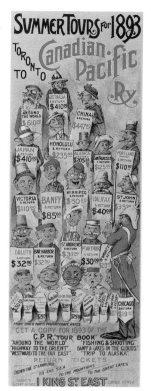

departure every three weeks. For $600 with everything included, a traveller could begin his voyage from Naples, a British port, or any city in Canada or the northern United States.

The "around the world" campaign paid off right away. The Transcanadian had never been so busy. The hotels were constantly full and others had to be built.

The Okanagan and Kootenay Valleys in British Columbia were perfect sites for summer resorts. Both had just been connected to the American border by a network of secondary rail lines and small ferry steamers that criss-crossed the surrounding lakes. These valleys became appealing stopovers on pleasant routes back to the United States. In 1894, two hotels opened, one at Sicamous, the other at Revelstoke. These establishments were similar to the other mountain hotels and offered the same relaxed atmosphere of a recreational vacation. Trout or salmon fishing and deer or goose hunting were only a few of the many activities possible in these splendid valleys dotted by deep emerald lakes.

At the same time a series of similar but smaller hotels sprang up further east: the Kaministiquia, a miniature version of the Vancouver Hotel, was built at Fort William in the Great Lakes region. Construction took place in New Brunswick as well.

One of the system's most beautiful gems was built in Quebec City. An arrival point for transaltlantic crossings and, since

the development of Pacific cruises, a gateway to Asia, Quebec had naturally become an important hub for tourists. Naturally enough, the idea of providing travellers with a luxury hotel cropped up and, in 1890, a group of businessmen undertook plans to build one. But economically, times were gloomy and the project was shelved until the city council got involved. It offered a ten-year tax exemption to any company that would build the hotel. Van Horne's ears pricked up. He created the Chateau Frontenac Company with a few shareholders, all of them more or less involved with the CPR.

The future hotel's name commemorated the Count of Frontenac who, renowned for both his glorious military career and his success with women at the French court, became governor of Quebec in 1672. The site chosen was no less prestigious. The hotel was built on the fortified heights of the city, on the spot where the Saint-Louis fortress once stood. On the edge of Dufferin Terrace, it overlooked the Saint Lawrence, Orleans Island, and Beaupré Hill. This ideal location raised the chateau to the rank of fortress. Once again, Van Horne's primary concern was to impress the visitor. In a letter to George Stephen he explained that he wasn't about to throw away money on "...marble and frills. Everything depends on broad effects, rather than ornamentation and details."

1. Around the world by rail and sea: a CPR advertisement, 1893. 2. A CPR poster advertising winter sports in Quebec and at the Château Frontenac, 1930. 3. The Hotel Sicamous reception desk in the 1920s.

Bruce Price was mindful of Van Horne's attitude when he drew up the plans. He designed a massive structure, faithful to the style already used at Banff. Once again, it was inspired by the French chateaux, especially Jaligny, whose robust architecture retained a medieval flavor.

The Chateau Frontenac was inaugurated in December 1893. This large building of red-orange brick imported from Scotland consisted of four wings laid out in a horseshoe shape. Its overall austerity was broken by a facade tower, corner turrets, and pointed gables. The dining and ball rooms, occupying two full floors, and the 170 bedrooms were appointed with Renaissance furniture, lending a touch of luxury and grandeur. The three symbolically-named suites in

the tower and turrets were the crowning glory of the hotel's success. The Quebec suite paid homage to the local population. The Chinese suite represented Quebec as a gate to the Orient. And the Dutch suite commemorated the origins of the CPR's first source of capital, unless Van Horne was honoring his own ancestors, as some people have insinuated.

The hotel, which could be seen from the river, became one of the city's major attractions; within six months it was completely booked up. In order to boost its capacity, Price added the Citadel Wing and the Pavilion in 1899. But the Frontenac didn't take on its present-day form until 1924 when a high central tower was added.

Encouraged by the Frontenac's success, the CPR's management decided to repeat the experiment in Montreal. This time, the company called on Price to design a train station-hotel complex on the Place Viger. Although it was

1. The Château Frontenac as seen from the Saint Lawrence in the 1890s. 2. A CPR poster from the 1930s: the Château Frontenac had become the symbol of Quebec City. 3. The cocktail hour in one of the Frontenac's lounges, 1930.

commonplace in Europe, this type of construction was unknown in Canada. The building, completed in 1898, was reminiscent of the Chateau Frontenac, but lighter and more graceful.

The Place Viger Hotel remained one of the most famous meeting places of Montreal society until the 1910s, when it was dethroned by the splendid Ritz-Carlton. The Ritz-Carlton was located in the center of Montreal's silk-stocking district: the Golden Square Mile, where 70% of all Canada's wealth

was said to be concentrated. Left on the sidelines and neglected, the Place Viger Hotel closed in 1933; the building, however, can still be admired today.

MRS. REED'S POPPIES

CPR hotels gradually began moving out from under the railroad's shadow around the turn of the century. Until then they had served as pretexts for stimulating rail traffic; now, little by little, they were becoming tourist attractions in their own right.

The CPR consequently decided to shift its promotional focus to the hotels themselves. The Algonquin Hotel in St. Andrews, New Brunswick, clearly illustrates this change. The company, which had never carried out a campaign in the Maritime Provinces, waited until it acquired the Algon-

quin in 1905 before promoting the region and its mild climate, beaches, and Bay of Fundy cruises.

One hotel's fame can spawn the success of another, even far away. When the Empress Hotel of Victoria (on Vancouver Island) was completed in 1908, the press immediately compared it to the Chateau Frontenac. These two hotels, gateways of the transcanadian route on opposite ends of the continent, became symbols. The first one's prestige contributed to make the second one renowned.

Like the Frontenac, the Empress occupied an impressive site. Facing the waterfront, it was built along the piers where the ferries linking the island port and the mainland docked. The chateau style was used once again. This time the plans were not drawn up by Price, who had died in 1903, but by a young architect named Francis Rattenbury. In 1892, Rattenbury had immigrated from England to British Columbia, where he designed the parliament buildings in Victoria. Although traces of Price's style can be found in the Empress, his successor's approach was more eclectic, lending the building a more authentically modern character. The chateau style reached its fullest, most mature expression in the Empress. Considerably enlarged in 1911 and 1928, the hotel's ivy-covered facade still keeps watch over the comings and goings of ships in the little port.

The CPR hotels were under the direction of the railroad's sleeping and dining car superintendent until 1902, but the expansion of the hotel network called for an autonomous organization. It was decided to create a Department of Hotels was created within the company; Hayter Reed, former manager of the Frontenac, was appointed director.

1. A CPR poster, 1935. 2. The CPR created Canada's luxury hotel industry, but rival establishments soon appeared offering comfortable rooms in elegant surroundings; here, elevators at Montreal's Ritz-Carlton, around 1930. 3. The Dufferin Terrace, which adjoins the Château Frontenac's structure and overlooks the Saint Lawrence.

Reed, a spirited, enthusiastic man in his fifties, had all the qualifications the position called for, plus one other great asset: a remarkable wife. This talented widow of a wealthy New York businessman had climbed her way to the summit of high society and become an authority on art and antiques. On her return to Canada in the 1880s, she

advised a number of collectors, including Van Horne (who had a passion for old china, among other things). No one was surprised when she began redecorating the Frontenac's over-solemn interior after her marriage to Reed in 1894, but she really won the hearts of the CPR in 1901, when the Duke and Duchess of Cornwall and York visited Canada. Mrs. Reed herself was put in charge of looking after these illustrious travelers, as well as furnishing and decorating the royal train. She aquitted the task so tactfully that from then on the company entrusted her with everything concerning the redecoration of its hotels.

Kate Reed traveled to Europe, especially to

1. The Algonquin, St. Andrew, New Brunswick, around 1950. 2. The Palm Room in Victoria's Empress Hotel; the large, multicolored skylight was concealed by a false ceiling until recent renovations restored it to its original grandeur. 3. The Empress and Victoria harbor, around 1920.

England, to pick out the tapestries, paintings, furniture, decorative objects, and antiques that would create or recreate the special mood of the CPR hotels. Her task was a tricky one: she had to find just the right balance between what had been agreed upon beforehand, the stilted taste of the Victorian bourgeoisie, and the ostentatious leanings of the American and Canadian nouveau riche. Playing on color harmonies, searching for the right details, matching fabrics and personally choosing the embroidered motifs on the table linen, she came up with a style that managed to be luxurious and domestic at the same time; a style which, in the end, made everyone feel at home.

The Place Viger Hotel was the first to be completely redecorated. Then it was time for the newcomers: the Empress Hotel of Victoria, of course, but also the Royal Alexandra in Winnipeg, built in 1904, whose stiff, unattractive architecture belied the

careful decoration of the interior. Finally, Kate Reed put her skills to work further west, taking on the "freshening up" of Banff Springs, Glacier House, Mount Stephen House, the Vancouver Hotel, and the Lake Louise Chalet, where she introduced the marvelous Iceland poppies which are there to this day, as famous as the lake itself.

KODAK AND THE INDIANS

Lake Louise owes the existence of its chalet (later baptised "chateau") to the lure of its spectacular setting. On a reconnaissance mission one fine summers's day in 1882, Tom Wilson, a guide attached to a railroad surveillance team, accidently discovered the lake the Indians called "the Lake of Little Fishes". Later renamed after Queen Victoria's

pers from Banff who did not want to miss out on an opportunity to admire the lake. By 1891 the CPR was thinking about laying a railroad extension from the trunk line. Two years later a new chalet replaced the original cabin, but even it proved too small to handle the steady stream of visitors. Latecomers were put up in tents whether they liked it or not. The CPR was finally convinced of the need for a real hotel.

In 1899 Rattenbury designed a new structure where the chateau style is again in evidence, but in this instance elements of mountain architecture were also employed, such as the extensive use of wood. In 1913, W.S. Painter, a student of Bruce Price and chief architect for the CPR since 1905, added a concrete wing whose terraced roof broke with the style traditionally used in the Rockies. In 1924, a terrible fire broke out, destroying Rattenbury's chalet. The only surviving structure was the "Painter wing", the oldest part of today's Chateau Lake Louise.

Like Lake Louise, all the mountain hotels were subject to constant renovation and expansion, which attests to the extraordinary vitality and powerful attraction of these establishments. Mount Stephen House was apparently enlarged around 1901. Glacier House, which had already been provided with an addition in 1889, was further enlarged in 1906 ; a new wing with 54 rooms and all the latest modern conveniences was built. The company paid particular attention to Banff Springs: the hotel was constantly being improved from 1902 to 1928, when a new hotel finally replaced the original one. Dominated by a central, eleven-story tower, the new structure brought to mind a gigantic manor house. The 1888 building had 250 rooms ; the new one, 600. This time the main influence was the somber, severe architecture of Scottish castles.

daughter, Princess Louise Caroline Alberta, this lake is exceptional both because of its location and the magnificent color of its water. Nevertheless, it failed to arouse the CPR's marketing sense. Not even Van Horne, with his uncanny flair for sniffing out success, was interested in the site. Until then no one had dreamed of building a hotel that wasn't near a railway station. The company was satisfied with a log cabin built in 1890 to accommodate overnight or day trip-

1. and 2. The dining room and lobby of the Royal Alexandra in Winnipeg, Manitoba. 3. Horsemen on the terrace of Château Lake Louise, about 1950. 4. Lady Aberdeen (wife of Canada's governor-general) drawing on the steps of the second Lake Louise chalet, 1894. 5. The famous poppies at Château Lake Louise.

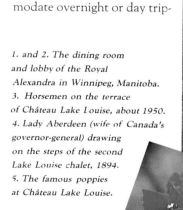

Despite the extensions

and renovations, the CPR hotels were still flooded by waves of tourists at the beginning of the century. Lack of space forced management to find all sorts of

alternative solutions, some of them rather unorthodox. Even after the addition of an extra wing, Glacier House was unable to cope with the increasing number of guests; sleeping cars had to be installed nearby. The Banff Springs Hotel, until then only open in the summer, was frequently forced to stay open an extra month in order to satisfy demand. It was even rumored that at Mount Stephen House the same room could be rented out to four people at the same time : if three of the guests were off on trips, the fourth one could use the room !

In fact, both the atmosphere and the nature of the tourists had greatly changed in the last fifty years. The good old, rough-and-tumble pioneering days of the railroad had given way to the era of organized group tours. The inhabitants of the Rockies

1. The Chalet Lake Louise in 1904; the hotel wasn't granted the title of "château" until 1925. 2. Afternoon tea at the Emerald Lake Chalet. 3. Chalet Lake Louise about 1915. 4. The fire which destroyed Rattenbury's building, Chalet Lake Louise, 1924.

were quick to understand that there was money to be made from the hordes of travelers as they alighted from their luxury-padded trains. The CPR encouraged all kinds of efforts to promote tourism, from stage coaches which met travellers at the station, to guided tours of

the neighboring lakes and forests on foot, horseback, or by car. The local Indian population decided to get in on the lucrative boom. Area tribes struck a deal with local "businessmen" and were soon being managed by the CPR itself. They staked their bets on the tourists' fascination for their culture. Each year large, traditional festivals were held where braves staged sham combats while their squaws sold exotic trinkets which couldn't be snatched up quickly enough.

To capture these unforgettable moments, tourists

feverishly clicked their Kodaks – that revolutionary, now indispensable instrument which prompted Lady Aberdeen to write, "American children learn kodaking long before they learn how to behave themselves".

THE NATIONAL TRIUMPH OF A STYLE

While the Canadian Pacific was consolidating its empire from coast to coast as well as abroad, other, more modest private companies plunged headlong into the great railroad adventure. The CPR's resounding triumph convinced competitors to build their own version of the chateau-hotel.

Around 1907 the New York architect Braford Lee Gilbert was commissioned to design a hotel-station complex in the young city of Ottawa. Until then the federal capital had only one acceptable though rather shoddy hotel called Russell House. There weren't even many public buildings, except for the imposing

mass of the copper-crowned Parliament, bristling with neo-Gothic flourishes and overlooking the Ottawa River and the mouth of the Rideau Canal. Gilbert's project echoed the haughty style of these buildings. But the president of the Grand Trunk Railroad objected; he insisted on a chateau. Gilbert was dismissed and the Montreal firm of Ross and MacFarlane landed the contract. The Chateau Laurier, named after the Prime Minister who had promoted the growth of the Grand Trunk, opened in June 1912. The granite, Italian marble, and Indiana yellow limestone ensemble combined elegance with restraint. A discreet facade contrasted with the ornamentation of the upper floors and with the gleaming copper-sheathed turrets and roof gables (copper had become the roofing material of all official or otherwise important buildings).

The chateau style was a tried and true formula for the deluxe hotel industry. Soon, the chateau Laurier had to be enlarged. This time the task was given to a new company, the Canadian National Railway, created in 1922 by the merger of several financially-troubled firms, including the Grand Trunk. A new wing was added to the Chateau Laurier between 1927 and 1929.

While Chateau Laurier

1. The Banff Springs Hotel in winter. 2. A movie being shot at the Banff Springs hotel in 1935; film crews often stayed at the hotel; in 1954, the Bow River Valley was the set for River of No Return; *it goes without saying that Marilyn Monroe, who broke a leg during the shooting, was particularly pampered by hotel waiters. 3. Facade of the Château Laurier, 1929.*

was under construction, the Grand Trunk was building other hotels. The Fort Garry Hotel in Winnipeg, Manitoba, was inaugurated in 1913; two years later the MacDonald Hotel in Edmonton, Alberta, was completed. Both were designed by Ross and MacFarlane, and they featured the same characteristics as the Ottawa palace: a sober treatment set off by an elaborate roof.

The Canadian National continued their activity in the hotel sector and opened the Bessborough Hotel in Saskatoon, Saskatchewan, in 1932. There, the abundance of turrets, dog-tooth moldings, and parapets ushered in a shift in architectural emphasis which would mark the 1920s and '30s. Chateau style attributes were deliberately

exaggerated through the extensive use of medieval details. Though the private sector was gradually abandoning this style, it became the emblem of government architecture, including that of the Canadian National Railway.

The CPR no longer used the chateau style, at least for its city hotels, even before its competitors had claimed it as their own. The Royal Alexandra in

Winnipeg, the Palliser Hotel in Calgary, built in 1914, and the 1927 Saskatchewan Hotel in Regina were built along lines similar to luxury hotels in the United States: cubic forms clad in a neo-classical sheathing. The "old" Vancouver Hotel, however, designed by Painter and Swales in 1916 and which replaced the original 1887 structure, defied any classification. Only Toronto's Royal York (1929) made some concessions to the chateau style: a small, pointed roof pierced by tiny dormer windows was perched on top of its enormous body. The reference was more explicit in the third Vancouver Hotel. Completed in 1939, this hotel was the offspring of a joint effort between the CPR and the Canadian National. Significantly, the architects were selected by the government-controlled Canadian National, rather than the privately-run CPR.

1. and 2. The entrance lobby and a revolving door of the Château Laurier. In the lobby alcove there is a bust of Wilfred Laurier, the first French Canadian prime minister. 3. Advertisement for the Palliser, Calgary.

The chateau style became "public property": it was embraced as Canadian national style, as the many designs proposed for the Confederation Building in Ottawa testify. The commission that judged the proposals in 1927 clearly stated, "All agree that the building should be Gothic in character; furthermore, as it is the general consensus of opinion that Gothic should be adopted to harmonize with the Parliament Buildings, being the type of architecture most suitable to our Northern climate, the Deputy Minister further recommends the adoption of the French chateau style of architecture of which the Chateau Laurier is a modernized type". Until the eve of the Second World War, any building calling for a measure of dignity or a sense of luxury – train station, post office, even an apartment building – was designed along these lines.

A certain rivalry with the U.S. no doubt encouraged the Canadian penchant for this new "national" style. The young nation had to affirm its identity in the face of its overbearing southern neighbor. The somber, massive forms of Canadian architecture are radically opposed to Washingtonian classicism.

A DREAM FULFILLED

When Canada's founding fathers chose as the country's motto *A mari usque ad mare* (from sea to sea), they were expressing a hope for the future rather than an existing reality. The builders of the nation's railways fulfilled their dream. The large chateau-hotels laid the foundations for a genuine Canadian national identity. They were the means by which visitors from around the world would discover the vast horizons of this new nation. But the adventure does not stop there; the Canadian Pacific Company has recently bought all the hotels previously managed by the Canadian National from the government. Chateau Lake Louise, Banff Springs, and the Chateau Frontenac are now under the same management as the Chateau Laurier and the Vancouver Hotel as well as more recent yet equally prestigious establishments such as the Queen Elizabeth in Montreal.

The symbolic merger of these two companies is the latest step in the work begun by Van Horne and all the others who strove with him to forge Canadian national unity.

1. Ottawa's Lord Elgin is not a CPR hotel but was nevertheless designed in the "chateau style". 2. The Jasper Park Lodge in Alberta was built in 1921 by the Grand Trunk Railroad; today it's part of the Canadian Pacific network. 3. One of the bar-restaurants at the Queen Elizabeth. 4. An annual celebration at the "Beaver Club", the prestigious restaurant in the Queen Elizabeth Hotel, built in 1958 and a favorite gathering place for Montreal's business community.

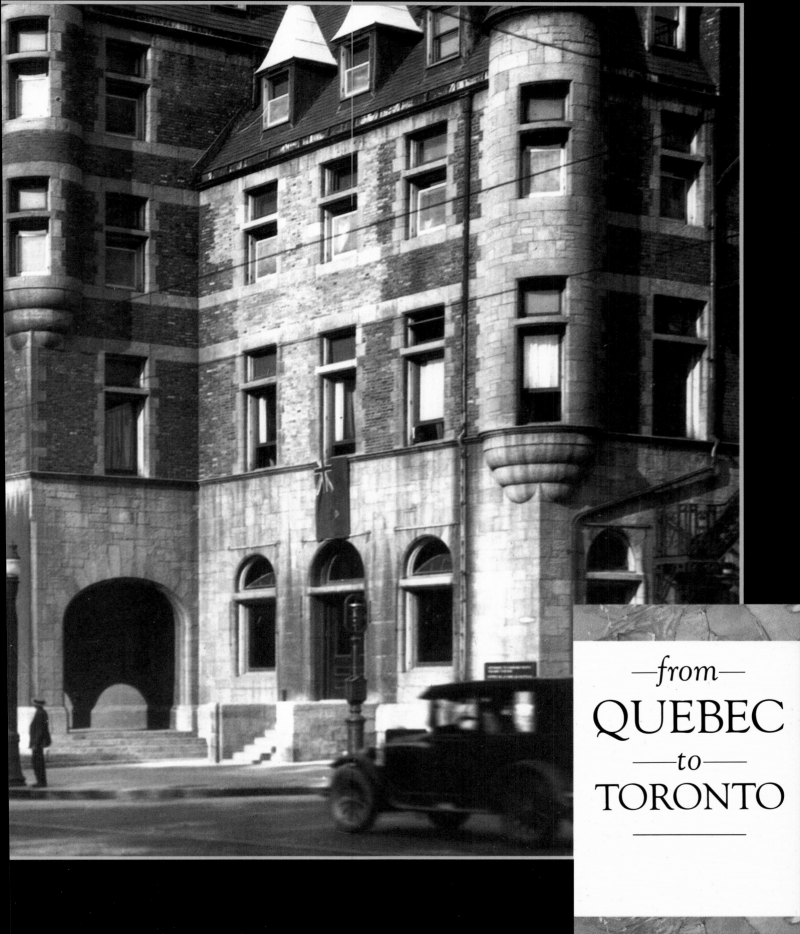

—from—
QUEBEC
—to—
TORONTO

Château Frontenac "can be seen from everywhere near and far. It's impossible to imagine the City's skyline without its silhouette, perched on the edge of a cliff overlooking the Saint Lawrence River. Its pale green roof, bell turrets, and jagged, fortress-like outline appear on the horizon, the crown jewel of this fluvial and maritime city... The view from my room on the thirteenth floor can keep me glued to the window for hours." Maurice Genevoix, *Canada*, 1945. ≃ Château Frontenac must be the only hotel in the world built on the site of a real fortress-castle. It has certainly lived up to the prestige of its glorious predecessor; during the Second World War, it was in the international spotlight twice: in August, 1943, and September, 1944 the "château" hosted the two "Quebec conferences", which brought together President Franklin Roosevelt, Prime Minister Winston Churchill, and the leaders of other allied nations. ≃ <u>Above</u>: the Salon Verchères, a luxurious landing leading to the ballroom, during the 1930s; a view of the château's facade in autumn. <u>Opposite</u>: a detail of the lobby. <u>Left page</u>: a vestibule on the ground floor. <u>Preceding pages</u>: the Place Viger Hotel, Montreal, in 1915.

"When the hotel's guests relaxed in the Salon Verchères - named after a heroine who lived in the days of Governor Frontenac - and feasted their eyes on the elegant arches, the potted palm trees, and the fountain shaped like an ancient Greek lamp, they got the impression that they were basking in a setting as refined as any the Governor himself could have offered." André Duval, 1979 ≃ <u>Above and right page</u>: a side view and detail of the Salon Verchères.

"A hotel like the Château Frontenac has everything it needs to host kings and their entourages, princes, prime ministers, cardinals... This hotel is where Ovide Plouffe showed up that evening, as stiff as a board in his perfectly-pressed tuxedo, with a dazzled Rita Toulouse holding on to his arm." Roger Lemelin, *La famille Plouffe*, 1948 ≃ Doormen and bellhops clad in epaulettes and gold braid endlessly criss-cross the Château Frontenac's lobby, one of the most bustling spots in Quebec. Elegant travellers, tour groups, and Americans seduced by the picturesque decor come and go in the soft light filtering through stained glass windows emblazoned whith coats of arms. Many visitors are also won over by the hotel's renowned split pea soup, which can be sampled at the "Café-Terrasse". The whirlwind doesn't die down until nightfall, a magic time for dinner accompanied by harp music, quiet conservations in peaceful surroundings, or an evening stroll on the Dufferin Terrace for a last leisurely look at the river. ≃ Above: a game being played in one of the château's lounges during the 1950s. Opposite: Château Frontenac seen from the Place Royale. Right page: a walk on the Dufferin Terrace.

Ever since the days when most of the travellers in *la belle province* used to be loggers, Quebec's hotel industry has been expanding, especially along the Saint Lawrence Seaway. The coming of steam boats and the sudden boom in seaway traffic resulted in a resort craze, and grand hotels sprang up wherever the vessels stopped off, from La Malbaie to Tadoussac. ≈ <u>Above</u>: the Manoir Richelieu. This hotel, located in Pointe-au-Pic on a clifff overlooking La Malbaie, opened in 1899. It was three stories tall, built entirely of wood, and covered with cedar-shingles. The original building was destroyed by fire in 1928 and replaced by a hotel in the then-popular château style. <u>Below and right</u>: facade of the Hotel Tadoussac; located where the Saint Lawrence and Saguenay Rivers meet, the hotel juts out over a sandy bay often filled with frolicking whales. The original building, constructed in 1864, was "one of the most beautiful, coolest, and most pleasant places imaginable" (Arthur Buies); torn down in 1941, the Canada Steamship Lines Company replaced it with the structure still standing today.

The best time to visit Château Montebello is winter. The snow-blanketed garden's crisp chill makes lazing around the main fireplace wonderfully cozy. The galleries, exposed-beam ceilings, and light shining through stained glass windows create an atmosphere of warmth and comfort. This log building dating from 1930 was originally built as a private club called the "Seigniory". Ten thousand red cedar beams were shipped from British Columbia for its construction. Hundreds of skilled craftsmen worked on the project, many of whom were brought in from Scandinavia because of their special talents and experience in this type of construction work. The building was completed in less than four months. It was turned into a hotel in 1970, when it was renamed the Château Montebello. ≃ Above: The participants in the 1981 economic summit meeting gather in the hotel's main lobby. The château has often been the scene of important international conferences because its remoteness simplifies the security mesures necessary for such occasions. Even though the hotel is off limits to the public during these events, the park that surrounds it still bustles with activity: security agents are perched in the trees and frogmen swim in the nearby river. Below: a room in 1930. Left page: the 27-meter tall fireplace in the central lobby, 1930.

One of the international elite's favorite forms of recreation during the 1930s was the "sporting vacation". Unlike many similar establishments, the Seigniory Club stayed open all year-round. Several of its rooms were devoted to various sports activities: for example, there is a swimming pool in a huge, cathedral-like space, and a curling court. But the Château Montebello's spectacular location continues to attract lovers of outdoor sports, too. Built on the banks of the Ottawa River, the hotel occupies the site of what was once a noble estate (hence the name "Seigniory Club"). It sits on an immense tract of land where guests can hike, golf, and hunt during the summer and ski and go sleigh-riding in winter. ≃ Above : the outdoor skating rink in 1930 ; and one of the entrances to the hotel. Opposite: an elegant club guest tries on a pair of skis, 1940. Right page: sun-bathing in the Seignory Club's garden, 1940.

The Ritz-Carlton, opened in 1913, was conceived and financed by six Montreal businessmen. It owes the first half of its name to the sumptuous hotel on the Place Vendôme in Paris and the second to London's famous Carlton. César Ritz agreed to loan his name to the new hotel as long as certain conditions were fulfilled: each room had to have a bathroom; each floor had to be endowed with a kitchen; and the dishes must not be "spoiled by strong sauces". In addition, the lobby's size had to both conform to certain dimensions and radiate a feeling of warmth and intimacy; and, last but not least, monumental interior staircases had to be built so that women in evening gowns could make spectacular entrances. Even today, it is quite fashionable to visit the Ritz-Carlton at tea time to sample the velvety scones served with real Devonshire cream. ≃ Above: the Hotel Windsor, another famous Montreal establishment, was the favorite residence of England's royal family when they visited Canada. Inset: a staircase in the Place Viger Hotel, around 1900. Opposite, right: a dining room in the Hotel Windsor. Left page: the Ritz-Carlton's facade in the 1910s.

Since Ottawa was chosen as Canada's capital in 1867, it has become a showcase for the Confederation. The city radiates a sense of calm, harmony, and well-being. In fact, some critics claim that life in the peaceful capital is downright boring. Whatever the case may be, the opening of the Château Laurier in 1912 was a major factor in establishing the city's pleasant atmosphere. The hotel not only provided tourists with a comfortable place to stay; it became a beloved landmark for Ottawa residents as well. A contest organised in 1987 in honor of the Château Laurier's 75th anniversary attested to the privileged place it still occupies in the hearts of the capital's residents. Invited to send in whatever souvenirs they had managed to collect over the years, they swamped the hotel with photographs, written material, and various items including ashtrays, glasses, an old spittoon, and even part of a plank from the old ballroom floor. The former owners of these "souvenirs" often sent along apologetic letters to excuse themselves for the little thefts that affection had led them to commit. ≈ Above: the ballroom during the 1910s, and the hotel orchestra around 1920. Opposite : in the early days the hotel offered water and electrotherapy cures; pictured here is the staircase leading to the pool and treatment rooms in 1930. Right page: detail of the facade.

The 1920s were a boom time for Canada, and the atmosphere in Toronto was dizzying. In 1927 the Prince of Wales inaugurated the city's monumental Union Station, as cavernous as a zeppelin hangar. Two years later the Royal York, the biggest hotel in the entire Commonwealth, opened. On that proud day, dancing went on until dawn in the four ballrooms specially decked out for the occasion. The hotel's managers handed out more than 1,200 gold fountain pens and powder boxes stamped with the hotel's arms to the glittering crowd. But the euphoria was short-lived; the year was 1929. Just a few months after opening day, hotel employees were combing the city looking for customers; a philanthropic millionaire threw a rain of dollars from the balustrade overlooking the central lobby. The Great Depression had begun. ≈ Above: the entrance to the main dining room (since renamed the Imperial Room) in the 1930s, and the hotel's facade. Opposite, right: the main entrance to the Royal York in the 1930s. Right page: the concert hall; the Imperial Room in the 1960s; reception lounge; lounge adjoining the main dining room in the 1930s.

When Toronto's City Hall moved to the western part of the city in 1899, George Gooderham, the richest man in town, was worried. He owned a distillery in the eastern part of Toronto, but the business quarter was sprouting up around the new municipal building. Not one to take things lying down, Gooderham had the idea of building a hotel in his own neighborhood in order to keep it economically vital. The King Edward Hotel was inaugurated in 1903. It reflected the splendor of the Edwardian Age, and the cream of Toronto society flocked to the "King Eddy". During the years immediately following its opening, visitors could catch a glimpse of figures like Kipling, Lloyd George, and the Archbishop of Canterbury. Perhaps even more picturesque were the gold prospectors from northern Ontario who would park their mules in the lobby before sampling oysters washed down with a 15-cent drink. Even though the King Edward fell on hard times during the Great Depression, today it is one of Toronto's most elegant and sought after hotel's. ≈ Above: Chef Fred Reindl with his crew, and the Victoria Room in 1940. Opposite: the "Mounties" at the entrance to the hotel. Left page: the actor Donald O'Connor lending a hand during the renovation of the ballroom.

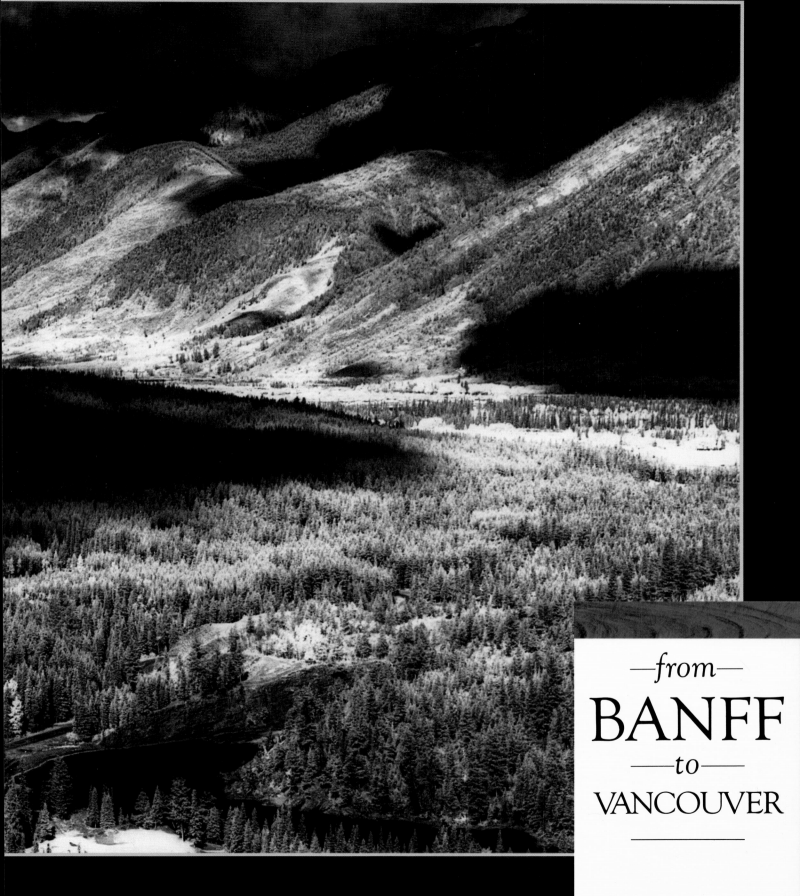

—from—
BANFF
—to—
VANCOUVER

"After a two-mile walk on a gorgeous path taking us through the village of Banff, across the Bow River, and through a beautiful forest criss-crossed by trails, we could make out the Banff Springs Hotel perched on the crest of a very high hill." A.B. Routhier, 1893. ≈ Above: the hotel lobby around 1890; the pillars and balustrades were in varnished red pine. Below: the north wing under construction in 1927; a wooden "cocoon" protected the construction site during the winter months. Right page: Swiss guides hired by the Canadian Pacific Railroad to accompany excursionists (the hotel can be seen in the background), 1915. Preceding pages: a bird's-eye view of the hotel and surrounding area.

From the very beginning, the Banff Springs Hotel made it a point to combine stylish elegance and casual friendliness. Distinguished visitors who had attended the evening chamber music recital were just as likely run into each other the next morning on the golf course or tennis courts. Still others would rather spend their time fishing, canoeing on the Bow River, or mountain-climbing. Visitors had even more ways to enjoy themselves. In the 1930s the annual "Indian Days" celebration provided yet another attraction. For the festival's inauguration ceremony, local tribes dressed in traditional costumes and paraded through the city streets before coming up the main avenue and gathering in the hotel's courtyard. ≈ Above: one of the Banff Springs Hotel promotional trademarks during the 1940s: a cowgirl and a "Mountie" ; and a Canadian Pacific Railroad advertisement. Below: the hotel golf course, 1930. Right page: an Indian brave posing in front of the Banff Springs Hotel.

"Of one or two places in the world it has been said that if we would but bide there a while we would see all our friends pass by. Of such and such a chair at the Café de la Paix in Paris that has been said, and of the Strand corner, in London, by Charing Cross. To the number of the places I would add the Banff Springs Hotel. Sit in the portico there, and in due time all your old friendships will be renewed." Comment of a member of English high society, London, 1937. ≈ <u>Above</u>: lounge in a suite, 1920s. <u>Inset</u>: the front portico with Brewster cabs, which brought guests to and from the Banff train station and took them on rides to marvel at the surrounding mountain scenery, around 1920. <u>Below</u>: an eighth-floor hallway, 1988. <u>Right page</u>: Canadian Prime Minister Mackenzie King with Queen Elizabeth and King George VI on the hotel's terrace, 1939; the British monarchs stayed in the Banff Springs two days. The hotel was decked out with huge wild flower wreaths for the occasion.

"Alone at Lake Louise, I sat on a bench in the 'château's' terraced gardens. As I watched dusk fall, the sun's dying rays reached the glaciers, caressed the tips of the majestic, densely-packed mountain peaks, brushed the snow, turning it pink, and finally faded away into the sky, like a puff of steam." Maurice Genevoix, *Canada*, 1945. ≈ <u>Above</u>: general view of Château Lake Louise as it was rebuilt after the 1921 fire; the Painter Wing survives but the graceful edifice designed by the architect Rattenbury has disappeared; the huge concrete structure erected to replace it was almost rejected by the National Parks commissioner; it was inaugurated in 1925. At the time, many people called the new building grim and forbidding. But the architecture itself was secondary: the hotel was conceived of as a gigantic observatory whose main purpose was to offer guests the eternal, natural spectacle of the lake and mountains. <u>Inset</u>: an advertisement for the Canadian Pacific Railroad (1938) and the pool (1930). <u>Right page</u>: a telescope on the veranda, 1930.

"I hope this little chalet never becomes a grand hotel and that the Canadian Pacific, which has already imported Swiss guides, never manages to lure the average tourist to the lovely banks of Lake Louise. That would desecrate one of the most marvelous sites in the New World, a place even Mr. Baedeker, happily, practically overlooked in his guide." Comments jotted down by the French Ambassador to Washington in the Lake Louise Guest Book, 1900. ≈ The Chalet Lake Louise did, however, expand into a grand hotel; today it boasts 520 rooms, feeds nearly 2,000 guests a day in high season, and stays open all year-round. But the French Ambassador's fears have turned out to be unfounded: the heavy flow of tourists has spoiled neither the atmosphere nor the setting. The vast yet warm interiors are still utterly charming and wearing a tie is still *de rigueur* at dinnertime. And Lake Louise still shimmers in all its timeless splendor beyond the main hall's bay windows. ≈ Above: detail of a hallway in the Painter Wing. Opposite and left page: a salon in the Glacier Wing, constructed in 1987. Preceding pages: hotel employees clear snow on the frozen lake's surface; hotel guests go skating on the lake at nightfall, warmed up by cups of steaming hot chocolate served around large burners.

"We're exhausted and the Hotel Vancouver is an immense black marble vault. It looks like a courtroom from the Great Beyond, designed to receive the accused and convicted. An intense feeling of abandonment and alienation sets in here ; this place feels like it's at the end of the earth." *Journal de Voyage*, Michel Tournier, 1977. ≈ Because of its mild climate, Vancouver is a favorite international vacation destination, but the city can feel like an ice-cold shower to the European just off the plane after a non-stop flight that began on the other side of the world. Vancouver's origins barely back a little more than a century, and first-time visitors are usually struck by two things. First, they're astonished by how new everything seems, but before they've even gotten over that impression, they're overwhelmed by the immensity of the open spaces surrounding the city. A vast, untouched wilderness comes right up to the edge of Vancouver; its presence and mystery seem to pervade every inch of the city. The gargoyles keeping watch on the roof of the Hotel Vancouver and the sculptures of outlandish creatures and Indian chiefs adorning the walls of the building's facade add a sense of magic to the place. This hotel is one of the most significant architectural landmarks in Vancouver, the stone-hard expression of an alliance between a breed of pioneers-builders and an ancient, legend-rich land. ≈ Above: a 1945 banquet in honor of the construction laborers who worked on the hotel. Left: the gargoyles. Right: cover of the Vancouver Sun from May, 1939. Below: one of the hallways off the hotel's rooms. Left page: the Hotel Vancouver.

T hree Vancouver Hotels followed one another in the heart of the city. The first one, built in 1888, was a graceless construction, but its porch was a popular gathering place. People came to relax in the cool breeze wafting over the veranda, as well as to catch a glimpse of celebrities passing by, from Rudyard Kipling to Sarah Bernhardt. The second Hotel Vancouver, opened in 1916, carried on the tradition, becoming the favorite meeting place for British Columbia's high society. The third hotel, still standing today, opened in May 1939. Like its predecessors, the new hotel instantly became the focal point for social activities in Vancouver. In all the major western Canadian cities, in fact, the "grand hotel" is still at the very heart of urban life. When the Empress of Victoria was closed for renovations in 1988, the island's residents worried about where to spend Christmas. The hotel's director saved the holiday spirit by announcing that the Hotel Vancouver would entertain the Empress Victoria's regulars. ≈ Above: foyer of the Grand Ballroom, and the "royal suites" floor, Hotel Vancouver. Opposite: souvenirs of Lord Mountbatten's Vancouver stay. Right page: The rotunda of the second Hotel Vancouver, closed in 1939, demolished in 1949.

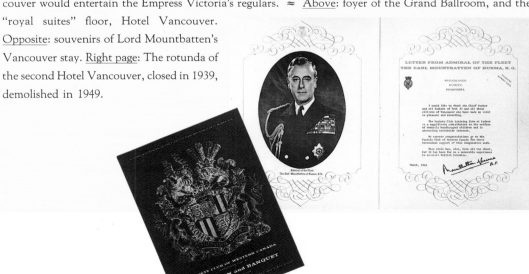

NORTHWEST TERRITORIES

Hudson Bay

CANADA

LABRADOR

BRITISH COLUMBIA

QUÉBEC

MANITOBA

SASKATCHEWAN

ALBERTA

Banff
Lake Louise

Vancouver

Lake Winnipeg

ONTARIO

New Brun

Seattle

Winnipeg

Québec
St-Lawrence

Bangor

WASHINGTON

Missouri

Montebello

Montréal

MAINE

Portland

MONTANA

NORTH DAKOTA

MINNESOTA

Ottawa

Lake Ontario

1

OREGON

IDAHO

Yellowstone
National Park

SOUTH DAKOTA

Minneapolis

St-Paul

WISCONSIN

Lake Superior

MICHIGAN

Lake Huron

Toronto

NEW YORK

2

Boston

3 4

WYOMING

Lake Michigan

Detroit

Buffalo

Lake Erie

5

Cleveland

New York

Sacramento

Virginia City

IOWA

NEBRASKA

Chicago

INDIANA

Columbus

OHIO

PENNSYLVANIA

Pittsburg

7

Philadelphia

6

Atlantic City

Berkeley

NEVADA

Yosemite National Park

UTAH

Glenwood
Springs

Boulder
Denver

Colorado

Cincinnati

WEST
VIRGINIA
Hot Springs

Washington

Baltimore

Cape May

San Francisco

CALIFORNIA

Colorado Springs

Kansas City

St-Louis

Ohio

VIRGINIA

White Sulphur
Springs

Richmond

COLORADO

KANSAS

MISSOURI

KENTUCKY

NORTH
CAROLINA

ATLA

Beverly Hills

Los Angeles

Riverside

ARIZONA

Phœnix

UNITED-STATES

Nashville

TENNESSEE

SOUTH
CAROLINA

OCE

San Diego

NEW MEXICO

Santa Fe

OKLAHOMA

Little Rock

Memphis

Mississippi

Atlanta

Charleston

ARKANSAS

ALABAMA

GEORGIA

PACIFIC

Dallas

MISSISSIPPI

OCEAN

TEXAS

St-Augustine

San Antonio

LOUISIANA

New Orleans

FLORIDA
Clearwater

St-Petersburg

Palm
Beach

Rio Grande

Hollywood
Boca Raton
Miami

Gulf of Mexico

1   VERMONT

2   NEW HAMPSHIRE

3   MASSACHUSETTS

4   RHODE ISLAND

MEXICO

5   CONNECTICUT

6   NEW JERSEY

7   MARYLAND

8   DELAWARE

0   500 km

BIBLIOGRAPHY

This is a selective bibliography of the major books dealing in general with American hotels or which include substantial information on that subject. For the most famous hotels, however, there also exist specific studies and brochures; for information on the publications dealing with them, contact the press service of the individual establishments.

The Grand Hotels of the United States
BLACKMAR, B., CROMLEY, E., EVERS, A. and HARRIS, N. *Resorts of the Catskills*, The Architectural League of New York, The Gallery Ass. of New York State, St. Martin Press, Inc., New York, 1979.

Chicago Architecture, 1872-1922 - Birth of a Metropolis, pp. 266 to 289, Exhibition catalog, The Art Institute of Chicago, Chicago, 1987.
CLEVELAND, A. *The Last Resorts*.
FERGUSON, N., LIMERICK, J. and OLIVER R. *America's Grand Resort Hotels*, Pantheon Books, New York, 1979.
GILMARTIN, G., MASSENGALE, J. and STERN, R. *New York 1900-Metropolitan Architecture and Urbanism 1890-1915*, pp. 252 to 305, Rizzoli International Publications Inc., New York, 1983.
GILMARTIN, G., MELLINS, T. and STERN, R. *New York 1930 - Architecture and Urbanism between the two World Wars*, pp. 201 to 225, Rizzoli International Publications Inc., New York, 1987.
HATTON, H. *Tropical Splendor-An Architectural History of Florida*, Alfred A. Knopf, New York, 1987.
WILLIAMSON, J. *The American Hotel, an anecdotal history*, Alfred A. Knopf, New York-London, 1930.

The Grand Hotels of Canada
BARRET, A. and WINDSOR LISCOMBE, R. *Francis Rattenbury and British Columbia Architecture and Challenge in the Imperial Age*, University of British Columbia Press, Vancouver, 1983.
CRUISE, D. and GRIFFITHS, A. *Lords of the Line*, Penguin Books Canada, Markham, Ontario, 1988.
DUBE, P. *Deux cents ans de villégiature dans Charlevoix*, Les Presses de l'Université Laval, Québec, 1986.
HARMON, C. and WHYTE, J. *Lake Louise, A Diamond in the Wilderness*, Altitude Publishing Ltd, Banff, 1982.
HART, E.J. *The Selling of Canada*, Altitude Publishing Ltd, Banff, 1983.
KALMAN, H.D. *The Railway Hotels and the Development of the Chateau-Style in Canada*, University of Victoria, 1968.
ROBINSON, B. *Banff Springs, The Story of a Hotel*, Summerthought Ltd, Banff, 1973.
Villégiature au Québec (La), Revue Continuité, n° 40, 1988.

PHOTO CREDITS

P. 146-147: The Bettmann Archive and, inset, Nevada Historical Society.
P. 148: above, The Bettmann Archive; center, Colorado Historical Society; inset, The Broadmoor Hotel.
P. 149: The Broadmoor Hotel; postcard, Colorado Historical Society.
P. 150-151: The Boulderado Hotel and Silvia Pettem.
P. 152: Aspen Historical Society.
P. 153: The Jerome and The Strater.
P. 154-155: The Brown Palace.
P. 156-157: The Oxford Alexis.
P. 158: above, The El Tovar; inset and below, The Arizona Biltmore.
P. 159: The Bishop's Lodge and The La Fonda.
P. 160-161: The Arizona Biltmore.
P. 162-163: Archives and Manuscripts Division of the Oklahoma Historical Society.
P. 164: above, The Bettmann Archive; inset, The St. Anthony Inter-Continental; below, The Lancaster.
P. 165: The Bettmann Archive.
P. 166-167: The St. Francis.
P. 168: above, Sirot-Angel; inset, The Sheraton Palace; below, The Bettmann Archive.
P. 169: Sirot-Angel.
P. 170 to 173: Anil Sharma.
P. 174-175: The St. Francis.
P. 176: The Biltmore Hotel (L.A.).
P. 177: above, Anil Sharma; center and below, The Biltmore Hotel (L.A.).
P. 178-179: The Biltmore Hotel (L.A.).
P. 180-181: Anil Sharma.
P. 182: above, Anil Sharma; inset and below, The Beverly Hills.
P. 183: Anil Sharma.
P. 184: The Bettmann Archive.
P. 185: above, left and below, The Royal Hawaiian Hotel; inset, The Moina Hotel; below (left), UPI/Bettmann Newsphotos.
P. 186: above, left, The Moana Hotel; right, Mr Desoto Brown/Bishop Museum;

below, all rights reserved.
P. 187: UPI/Bettmann Newsphotos.
P. 188-189: The Royal Hawaiian Hotel.
P. 190: CP Rail Corporate Archives.
P. 191: 1. and 2. CP Rail Corporate Archives; 3. Whyte Museum of the Canadian Rockies.
P. 192: 1. National Gallery of Canada; 2. and 3. CP Rail Corporate Archives.
P. 193: 4. CP Rail Corporate Archives; 5. Notman Photographic Archives.
P. 194: 1. National Gallery of Canada; 2. all rights reserved.
P. 195: 1. all rights reserved; 2. and 3. CP Rail Corporate Archives.
P. 196: 1.2.3. CP Rail Corporate Archives.
P. 197: 1.2.3. CP Rail Corporate Archives.
P. 198: 1. and 3. CP Rail Corporate Archives; 2. Catherine Donzel.
P. 199: 1. and 3. CP Rail Corporate Archives; 2. Archives of the Canadian Rockies.
P. 200-201: CP Rail Corporate Archives.
P. 202: CP Rail Corporate Archives.
P. 203: 1. CP Rail Corporate Archives; 2. The Ritz Carlton; 3. Catherine Donzel.
P. 204: CP Rail Corporate Archives.
P. 205: CP Rail Corporate Archives; 5. Carole Harmon.
P. 206: 1.2.3. CP Rail Corporate Archives; 4. Whyte Museum of the Canadian Rockies.
P. 207: 1. Catherine Donzel; 2. CPR Corporate Archives; 3. Chateau Laurier.
P. 208: 1.2. Catherine Donzel; 3. The Palliser.
P. 209: 1. The Lord Elgin; 2. CPR Corporate Archives; 3.4. The Queen Elizabeth.
P. 210-211: CP Rail Corporate Archives.
P. 212: Catherine Donzel.
P. 213: above, The Bettmann Archive; inset, The Chateau Frontenac; below, Catherine Donzel.
P. 214-215: Catherine Donzel.
P. 216: above, CP Rail Corporate

Archives; below, The Chateau Frontenac.
P. 217: Catherine Donzel.
P. 218: above, The Manoir Richelieu; below, Continuité/Brigitte Ostiguy.
P. 219: Continuité/Brigitte Ostiguy.
P. 220: CP Rail Corporate Archives.
P. 221: above, The Chateau Montebello; below, CP Rail Corporate Archives.
P. 222: above and below, The Chateau Montebello; inset, Catherine Donzel.
P. 223: The Chateau Montebello.
P. 224: The Ritz-Carlton, Montreal.
P. 225: above, CP Rail Corporate Archives; inset, CP Rail Corporate Archives; below, Sirot-Angel.
P. 226: The Chateau Laurier.
P. 227: Catherine Donzel.
P. 228: above, The Bettmann Archive; below, CP Rail Corporate Archives.
P. 229: above, The Bettmann Archive; center, The Royal York; below, The Bettmann Archive.
P. 230-231: The King Edward.
P. 232-233: CP Rail Corporate Archives.
P. 234: above, CP Rail Corporate Archives; below, Whyte Museum of the Canadian Rockies/Byron Harmon Photograph Coll.
P. 235: Whyte Museum of the Canadian Rockies/Byron Harmon Photograph Coll.
P. 236-237: CP Rail Corporate Archives.
P. 238: above and inset, Whyte Museum of the Canadian Rockies/Byron Harmon Photograph Coll.; below, Catherine Donzel.
P. 239: CP Rail Corporate Archives.
P. 240: above, The Bettmann Archive; inset and below, CP Rail Corporate Archives.
P. 241: Whyte Museum of the Canadian Rockies/Byron Harmon Photograph Coll.
P. 242 to 245: Catherine Donzel.
P. 246-247: The Hotel Vancouver.
P. 248: above, Catherine Donzel; below, The Hotel Vancouver.
P. 249: The Bettmann Archive.

ACKNOWLEDGEMENTS

We would especially like to thank Mr Plouseau, director of the Claridge-Bellman Hotel in Paris who has been of the utmost help and encouragement from the very first volume of this series on international hotels. We would also like to express our gratitude to Mr. David Greenstein, director of the Bettmann Archives in New York, who was instrumental in helping us assemble the illustrations used in this book.

THE GRAND HOTELS OF THE UNITED STATES

We would like to thank all of the hotels that made their archives available to us and, in particular: the Ambassador East and Sheila King (Public Relations); the Belvedere and Stacey L. Hostetler; the Biltmore of Los Angeles and both Victoria King and Holly Barnhill; the Blackstone; the Boulderado and Silvia Pettem; the Brown and Vicki Godbey (Director of Public Relations); the Chicago Hilton and Towers and Kit Bernardi (Director of Public Relations); the Drake; the Fairmont of New Orleans and John DeMers (Director of Public Relations); the Halekulani; the Hotel Inter-Continental New York and both Dagmar Woodward (Resident Manager) and Melanie S. Illian (Director of Public Relations); the Jefferson Sheraton Hotel and Ms Cruickshank; the Jerome and Beth Mitchell (Director of Marketing and Public Relations); the Mayflower and Bernard C. Awenenti (General Manager); the Moana; the Oxford Alexis and Nancy Cameron; Palmer House and Ken Price (Director of Public Relations); the Pierre; the Plaza; the Ritz Carlton of Boston; the St. Francis; the Seelbach; the Sheraton-Palace Hotel; the Strater and Kristi Nelson (Director of Sales); the Timberline Lodge; the Waldorf-Astoria.

THE GRAND HOTELS OF CANADA

This chapter could never have been written without the kind cooperation of Canadian Pacific Hotels & Resorts and their representatives. Special thanks go to Robert S. DeMone, Chairman, President & Chief Executive Officer of this hotel chain; to Walter Borosa, Director of Public Relations, and to Anyck Turgeon whose kindness and efficiency we highly appreciated during our entire stay in Canada. We would also like to thank all of the Canadian hotels who welcomed us and made their archives available to us: the Banff Springs Hotel and both Fritz Koeppel (General Manager) and Marilyn Bell (Administrative Assistant to the Vice President); the Chateau Frontenac and Isabelle Duchesneau (Assistant Manager and Guest Relations); the Chateau Lake Louise and Wendy Lash (Public Relations); the Chateau Laurier and both Peter H. Howard (General Manager) and Sotiri Vaos (Executive Assistant Manager); the Chateau Montebello and Jacques Ternois (Executive Assistant Manager); the Empress and Ian Barbour (General Manager); the Palliser and R.P. Thompson (General Manager); the Queen Elizabeth and Caroline DesRosiers (Director of Public Relations); the Royal York and Timothy Whitehead (Vice President and General Manager); the Hotel Vancouver and Deborah Upton (Director of Public Relations).

Lastly, we would especially like to thank Nancy Williatte-Battet, who made the CP Rail archives available to us and furnished us with much invaluable information. Thanks, also, to Nadine Beauthéac, Patrick Bouchard de Montmorency, David Mendel and Paul Trépanier (Editor in Chief of "Continuité").

Concept: Catherine Donzel and Marc Walter.
Art direction: Marc Walter.
Picture research and captions: Catherine Donzel.
Adaptation for the English language: Glenn Naumovitz
and Philip and Mary Hyman.
Printed and bound in Italy by G.E.P.